Hands-on Programmatic In-house Digital Advertising

Learn Data Design, AI Implementation, Bidding Strategies, and Strategic Thinking

Raghavendra Agarwala

www.bpbonline.com

FIRST EDITION 2022
Copyright © BPB Publications, India
ISBN: 978-93-91030-193

LIMITS OF LIABILITY AND DISCLAIMER OF WARRANTY

To View Complete
BPB Publications Catalogue
Scan the QR Code:

Dedicated to

My beloved Parents:

Dr. Vijaya Agarwala
Dr. R.C. Agarwala

&

My wife Smita and
My Daughters Shivalika and Vedika

About the Author

I am **Raghavendra Agarwala,** commonly addressed by Raghu. I have been working with professional software development since 1995. I have rich experience of 18 years in the mobile marketing and digital advertising industry. Over a while, I have designed and sometimes coded Content Management Systems, Service Delivery Platforms, Data Pipe Platforms, Bidders, Biddable Media Exchanges, Customer Data Platforms, Data Management platforms and related systems.

About the Reviewer

Kanika Bhandari is a professional Digital Marketing Strategist who's primary goal is teach people about the power of Digital marketing. She has a total of 7 years of experience in the digital industry and is also a successful Udemy Instructor. Her hands on marketing experience has helped her to gain a deep knowledge about the most modern marketing techniques. She loves talking and teaching about Programmatic Advertising, SaaS marketing, OTT advertising etc. Passionate about digital marketing, Kanika is now working as an independent consultant and has benefitted numerous clients with her deep knowledge.

Her career is a blend of Sales, marketing and analytics. As a sales person she has helped a lot of small business clients to grow their sales by 15%, month on month basis. With her amazing marketing style she has consulted a lot of SaaS clients to create a super buzz in Prelaunch phase.

In her spare time, Kanika enjoys reading, trekking and cooking.

Acknowledgement

There are a few people I want to thank for the continued and ongoing support they have given me during the writing of this book. First and foremost, I would like to thank my father for continuously encouraging and pushing me for writing the book — I could have never completed this book without his support. I also want to thank my colleagues Rishi, Rohit and Garvit who supported me on this journey. I also would want to thank my industry friends who helped me to constantly focus and navigate through tricky topics.

My gratitude also goes to the team at BPB Publications for being supportive enough to provide time and give rather quick responses. I also would like to thank Nrip who seeded the idea and gave me enough comfort to pursue on this journey.

Finally, I thank everyone who encouraged me. It was a much tougher undertaking than I initially imagined. I feel great that finally, I will be able to contribute to the ecosystem that has given me a livelihood.

Preface

This book tries to cover all the aspects of programmatic in-housing. It is designed to help understand the different building blocks in the ecosystem. The reader will find that the chapters are independent in their context and as a whole one can get a good head start to implement an in-housing project. In general, the book is designed to help architects, business analysts and possibly C-Level executives in exploring the options around solutions and services. I have purposely kept the buy and sell side of the aspect together so that one can understand both sides of working.

Chapter 1, Cookies and other IDs: Cookies and ID mechanics are the primary sources of identifying, tracking and targeting a user. The whole world of internet IDs working around cookies and device ID(GAID/IDFA and so on). It becomes imperative to understand the basic working before getting into more advanced topics. Having said that ID mapping is a very technical aspect of the programmatic ecosystem. For a more business-focused approach, one can easily skip this chapter and still would be able to make sense of the rest of the book.

Chapter 2, Data and AI Strategies: Everyone knows that data is oil but few know that it's crude oil. It takes a lot of effort to structure it, process it and finally derive some value out of it. This chapter helps to provide a sense of the data sources that are available, their place in the ad-tech data universe, some sample processes and some AI implementations. The idea is to look at data in terms of value. This become one of the most important chapters and it's also a precursor to Chapter 3 working of CDP & DMP.

Chapter 3, Working of DMP and CDP: DMP and CDP help in data acquisition, arrangement, grouping, indexing and AI/ML model processing etc. CDP and DMP bring methods in the madness of the data. The chapter helps in the understanding of the construct and the use-cases that it helps in the ad-tech ecosystem.

Chapter 4, Exchanges, Ad-Servers and Header Bidding: Helps understand the various monetization stack from the publisher's perspective. These systems are necessary for revenue maximization. The programmatic ecosystem is fairly complex and the understanding of how different pieces fit becomes essential. A must-read for all publishers.

Chapter 5, Bidders and Meta DSP: Helps us understand the various media buy components, tools and platforms. Media buying requires can be done via different bidding strategies. It's important to understand how these things work to be able to design, implement and use them optimally. It's a must for all Brands that do programmatic buying.

Chapter 6, Data Privacy by Design: Ad-Tech revolves around data and data revolves around user privacy. It's important to understand the GDPR paradigm and the idea behind it to be able to handle data flows for digital advertising. Privacy also can determine the number of options. This is a must for brands and publishers.

Chapter 7, In-housing - The way forward: Provides a high-level view of the in-housing and how one can connect all the dots in the ecosystem. It prepares the reader to undertake the in-housing journey.

Downloading the code bundle and coloured images:

Please follow the link to download the
Code Bundle and the *Coloured Images* of the book:

https://rebrand.ly/771465

Errata

We take immense pride in our work at BPB Publications and follow best practices to ensure the accuracy of our content to provide with an indulging reading experience to our subscribers. Our readers are our mirrors, and we use their inputs to reflect and improve upon human errors, if any, that may have occurred during the publishing processes involved. To let us maintain the quality and help us reach out to any readers who might be having difficulties due to any unforeseen errors, please write to us at :

errata@bpbonline.com

Your support, suggestions and feedbacks are highly appreciated by the BPB Publications' Family.

Did you know that BPB offers eBook versions of every book published, with PDF and ePub files available? You can upgrade to the eBook version at www.bpbonline.com and as a print book customer, you are entitled to a discount on the eBook copy. Get in touch with us at :

business@bpbonline.com for more details.

At **www.bpbonline.com**, you can also read a collection of free technical articles, sign up for a range of free newsletters, and receive exclusive discounts and offers on BPB books and eBooks.

BPB is searching for authors like you

If you're interested in becoming an author for BPB, please visit **www.bpbonline.com** and apply today. We have worked with thousands of developers and tech professionals, just like you, to help them share their insight with the global tech community. You can make a general application, apply for a specific hot topic that we are recruiting an author for, or submit your own idea.

The code bundle for the book is also hosted on GitHub at **https://github.com/bpbpublications/Hands-on-Programmatic-In-house-Digital-Advertising**. In case there's an update to the code, it will be updated on the existing GitHub repository.

We also have other code bundles from our rich catalog of books and videos available at **https://github.com/bpbpublications**. Check them out!

PIRACY

If you come across any illegal copies of our works in any form on the internet, we would be grateful if you would provide us with the location address or website name. Please contact us at **business@bpbonline.com** with a link to the material.

If you are interested in becoming an author

If there is a topic that you have expertise in, and you are interested in either writing or contributing to a book, please visit **www.bpbonline.com**.

REVIEWS

Please leave a review. Once you have read and used this book, why not leave a review on the site that you purchased it from? Potential readers can then see and use your unbiased opinion to make purchase decisions, we at BPB can understand what you think about our products, and our authors can see your feedback on their book. Thank you!

For more information about BPB, please visit **www.bpbonline.com**.

Table of Contents

CHAPTER 1
Cookies and Device IDs

Introduction

In today's age, the Internet is an envelope full of opportunities. Earlier, it was about surfing the internet, but as we are progressing and learning more each day, we are getting to know that we can monetize our presence on the internet as well. This is only possible through the advertising industry. The advertising industry is evolving rapidly with the introduction of new methodologies of advertising. Digital advertising is experiencing a period of bloom because of consumers spending more of their time on digital media. Consumers want everything to be hassle-free and easily available at their doorstep, without the need to physically go out to fetch anything. Because of this evolution on the part of consumers' end, the marketers are making the options available through a click. The ad-tech world primarily consists of the audience and the media. The core of an audience is the ID mechanism that it uses. A part of the ID mechanism is driven by the http protocol, and another part is driven by ad-tech business models in play. The advent of the audience goes in line with "data is the new oil," wherein the oil industry is very well regulated. Some of the restrictions that are tech generated are mostly put forth by Apple and Google, who own large browser pieces and continue to make changes even when they are in the best interest of the consumers. They are constantly creating disruptive changes for the other stakeholders due to this variable behavior.

Structure

- Working of cookies

- Working with cookies and device IDs

- The first-, second-, and third-party cookies

- Cookie syncs

- ID maps between DSP/bidder, DMP, and Exchanges

- Impact of deprecation of third-party cookies

Objective

This chapter is meant to provide an insight into the ad-tech aspect of cookies and device IDs. The idea is to make the readers aware of the depths at which these IDs impact the flow and also the control a developer can exercise while working with them. In some of the portions of this chapter, I have tried to add some code snippets. The in-depth working of the code is purposely kept out of the scope to cover the ad-tech part. Understanding how a cookie works is very crucial in the ad-tech world. Working of cookies touches the aspects of user privacy, prospecting, retargeting, activation of data, and so on. As most of these are moving wheels of a core, understanding and building the blocks piece-by-piece would help in comprehending the current scenarios and also possibly the future ones.

Working of cookies

Cookies are persistent variables that can be stored while a user is browsing through the Web (browser and Web apps). The website will ask for the user's consent to store data. Once a user accepts, it means the cookies are storing information for future preferences and suggestions. If a user denies it, that means the website cannot store any such information. They are domain-specific variables and can be accessed by the domain page. There are many uses of a cookie, but we will mainly focus on the ad-tech part of it.

In ad-tech, both programmatic and ad-network use the user ID mechanisms for the audience play. Users are identified in various formats such as the Web, mobile Web, and apps.

> **Note: Audience play refers to user targeting and behavior tracking. User tracking is done via page load, click, impression, article read, sign in/login, and so on.**

The two preventive measures that can be taken to manage an ID are via cookies on the Web, mobile Web, and device ID on apps. Apps can further use **Google**

Advertising ID (GAID) for android-based devices and Identifier for Advertising (IDFA) for iOS-based devices. Because of the presence of these, users can opt-out of the tracking done by the advertisers in their device settings.

In today's ad-tech ecosystem, multiple ad-tech stakeholders are present. They are as follows:

- **Publisher ad-server**: Typically a publisher-side ad system helps in configuring ad-units, handling direct demand, and generating ad-requests.

- **Exchange**: It plays an important role in conducting auctions.

- **Bidder/Demand-Side Platform (DSP)**: A bidder is the core component of any programmatic demand-side platform. It is primarily responsible for allowing buyers of digital advertising inventory to preside over multiple ad exchange and data exchange accounts through one interface.

- **Data Management Platform (DMP)**: A DMP is essentially used for data synchronization between various modules within the ecosystem, including the publisher and the advertiser.

- **Customer Data Platform (CDP)**: A CDP is a next-generation DMP that picks up features from **Customer Relationship Management** (CRM). In ad-tech, a CDP is focused on buying media, selling media, and data trading.

- **Click tracker**: It tracks the click that is responsible for the traffic control between various sites.

- **Attribution**: It helps the marketer to attribute an event to various channels.

All these systems will drop second- or third-party cookies aimed at user tracking. There are many other systems in the ad-tech ecosystem for fraud detection, DCO, and so on, but we will focus on systems that are dropping cookies from an ad-tech perspective.

Working with cookies and device ID

Cookies can be classified into blocks. Firstly, a cookie is dropped on the domain of the same domain. Secondly, a cross-domain cookie is dropped by the respective domain that is initiated by the domain. Examples are as follows:

- a.com drops a cookie with a.com domain
- a.com drops a cookie with b.com domain

The commonly used mechanism to set and get a cookie is via JavaScript.

For example:

```
Drop Cookie //
function setCid(id){
    var cname =»_tai»;
    var cvalue = id;
    var exdays=30;
    var d = new Date();
    d.setTime(d.getTime() + (exdays*24*60*60*1000));
    var expires = «expires=» + d.toGMTString();
    document.cookie = cname + «=» + cvalue + «;» + expires +»;path=/»;


}


Read Cookie //
function getCid(){
  var name =  « _tai=»;
  var ca = document.cookie.split(‹;›);
  for(var i = 0; i < ca.length; i++) {
      var c = ca[i];
        console.log(«value of c : ", c);
    while (c.charAt(0) == ‹ ‹) {
      c = c.substring(1);
     }
    if (c.indexOf(name) == 0) {
        console.log(«index : «, c.substring(name.length, c.length));
      return c.substring(name.length, c.length);
     }
  }
  return «nocid»;
}
```

However, a cookie can also be set via a backend http-based **Application Programming Interface (API)**, but this becomes limited to the same domain. Nevertheless, there are significant advantages of using it away from the performance aspect.

Drop Cookie:

```
  public static void dropCookie(HttpServletRequest request,
HttpServletResponse response,
```

```
                       String cName, String tp_id, String domain)
{
try

      {
              String cookieValue =    tp_id;
              Cookie = new Cookie("_tai_"+cName,cookieValue);
              cookie.setDomain(Configuration.cookie_domain);
              cookie.setPath("/");
              cookie.setMaxAge(60 * 60 * 24 * 365 +
(60 * 60 * 24 * 334) ); //cookie expiration time for 1 years and 11
months in the future
              response.addCookie(cookie);
      }
catch(Throwable e)
{
              e.printStackTrace();

      }
}
```

Read Cookie:

```
 public static String readCookie(HttpServletRequest request,  String
cName)
{
Cookie[] cookieList = request.getCookies() ;
String cookie = null;
UserTracker.infoLog.debug("cookie name:: " + "_tai_"+cName);
try
{
              if(cookieList != null)
              {
                    for (int i =0; i< cookieList.length; i++)
                    {
Cookie coo = cookieList[i] ;
if(coo.getName().equalsIgnoreCase( "_tai_"+cName))
{
                              cookie = coo.getValue();
                              }
```

```
                    }
                }
}catch(Exception e)
{
e.printStackTrace();
}
return cookie;
}
```

Note: The sample code is an embedded Java Jetty-based code. You may need to initiate a socket and an http handler to use the preceding methods.

The device ID is typically accessible from the app **Software Development Kit (SDK)** to the program. All the apps on a handset can use this ID. This eliminates the need to sync up the ID and can be readily used in ad-serving. This also means that there is no need of setting up the ID. The way to access the device ID is as follows:

```
<Android code snippet>
```

```
<Apple code snippet>
```

One can check for the cookie that has been set for the domain from the browser:

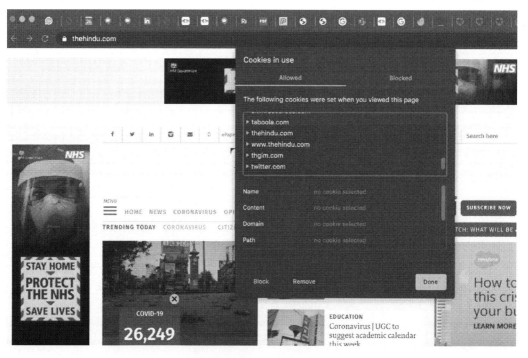

Figure 1.1: Cookies being dropped from various domains

The first-, second-, and third-party cookies

The first-, second-, and third-party cookies essentially form the ownership paradigm. The ownership of cookies also percolates to the regulatory obligations. For example, if a user lands on a.com, then a.com, under General Data Protection Regulation (GDPR), is required to protect the user's rights. However, in ad-tech format, third-party cookies are used for tracking and targeting purposes. Nevertheless, in the new regime, a.com is supposed to track second- and third-party cookies. All other applications of reporting, ticketing, and so on will be built on this, ensuring a tight control on cookie drops that are initiated by a.com.

In today's ad-tech environment where multiple stakeholders want to track users to server ads, third-party cookies have become essential for audience tracking.

The first-, second-, and third-party data will be covered in *Chapter 2, Data and AI Strategies*. As cookies are the anchor of the data generally, they are also referred to similarly:

- A first-party cookie is dropped when a user comes to `a.com,` and `a.com` internally drops a cookie on the same domain.

- A second-party cookie is dropped when a user comes to `a.com` and `b.com`, a cookie is dropped in the `a.com` domain.

- A third-party cookie is dropped when a user comes to `a.com` and the user is redirected to b.com, and b.com drops a cookie of `b.com`.

These mechanisms become more imperative to the working of cookie mechanics. In the case of the incognito mode, the browser does not allow the dropping of any cookies.

There also certain variables that help in controlling the access control of these cookie flows:

- **Access-control-allow-credentials**: This parameter communicates to a browser to expose cookies or a TLS certificate. CORS does not include cookies, but with client and server settings, this can be achieved. Some DMPs also use the JSON-P method to drop cross-domain cookies (that is, third-party cookies), which can lead to vulnerability. This is also called cross-site request forgery, or in short known as CSRF.

- **Access-control-allow-headers**: This parameter is used to secure the http headers by stating what parameters are allowed in the header.

- **Access-control-allow-methods**: This is used via preflight requests to ensure the sanctity of the methods that are being used.

- **Access-control-allow-origin**: It validates if the response that has been requested can be shared with the origin.

- **Cross-Origin Resource Sharing (CORS)**: It uses the http header to allow Web applications using one origin to share resources between other domains.

These parameters have complex implementations and repercussions. It is imperative to understand them before working with a cookie. The implementation itself is kept out of the scope of this book. Also, there is much more control that can be attained via a proxy, but that is out of the scope for this book as well.

As cookies can also be used for storing data beyond IDs, it can also become a security risk. Hence, a tight control is mandatory here.

Cookie syncs

Cookie syncs are required to share data between two data owners. Technically, this boils down to two domains being able to track users between them. From a bird's eye view, if I say there are ten publishers and/or advertisers who wish to track a user between them, then all of them need to sync cookies between them. Usually, this is done using a third-party cookie that anchors all of them.

There are two ways to sync cookies. For example, there are two domains, namely **a.com** and **b.com**:

- **User comes to a.com**: **a.com** drops a cookie with ID "**acom**" and then redirects the user to **b.com** with URL or post-parameter set as "**acom.**" Further, **b.com** drops a cookie "**bcom**" and maintains an ID map at **b.com**'s end where the "**acom<->bcom**" map is maintained.

- **User comes to a.com**: **a.com** drops a cookie "**acom**" and redirects to **b.com** with a token. Further, **b.com** drops a cookie "**bcom**" and passes the value "**bcom**" and the token S2S call to **a.com**. Here, a.com maintains an ID map of "**acom<->bcom.**"

This is the underlying mechanism for any two systems to come in sync. Depending on the application flow, one of the forementioned is chosen. The said process does not require any third-party cookie. However, when multiple publishers, advertisers, and ad-tech systems want to sync together, then an easier way to make that happen is by using an anchor cookie. With this mechanism, one can just sync their cookie with this anchor cookie, and the anchor cookie can enable all data at all relevant places.

This fundamental aspect of anchor cookies is also used by CDPs and DMPs for data activation. Not to mention that cookie sync is used by all ad-tech stakeholders in some or the other format.

ID maps between DSP/bidder, DMP, and exchanges

The base protocol of **Real-Time Bidding** (RTB) was designed to trade media and data. However, most of the **Supply-Side Platforms** (SSPs) that originated from ad-networks were never meant to trade data. The legacy continued, and even though the exchange to DSP communication is fully RTB compliance, the publisher to exchange traffic is still ad-request based and usually bears no audience data. This went nicely with Google's agenda who never wanted to share user data with anyone. The combination of the tech, based on cookie sync, and the business intent led to the advent of DMP's coming into the RTB scene.

In the current scenario, the first-party cookie is never used for ad-serving. This becomes a problem for compliance as it reduces the work for a publisher to sync cookies with other ad-tech players.

A DMP usually syncs between the publishers, advertisers, and other data owners and makes the audience available to the marketer via the DSP/bidder.

On the other hand, the exchange usually has deep integration with the publisher. The exchange usually governs the rendering and user tracking on the publisher sites. It gets ad-requests from publishers and sends them to the bidders. We will discuss this in the latter part of the book. From an ID perspective, as every bidder also hosts its audience for targeting and is synced with the exchange, this means that it has to maintain ID maps for all the bidders that are attached to it. So, when an exchange has to send out bid requests to the bidder, it uses the respective cookie IDs (CID) on a per bidder basis.

Figure 1.2: ID placements at various levels

There are scenarios where there is DMP–DMP sync and exchange–exchange sync that makes them much more complex. They all work with the underlying sync process.

The various ID maps that exist in today's ecosystem are as follows:

- DSP-initiated and DSP store the map table
- DSP-initiated and exchange store the map table

- Exchange-initiated and exchange store the map table

- Exchange-initiated and DSP store the map table

The cookie sync and map tables have many flavors. In many ways, it also has legacy baggage that the ecosystem has to carry; so many times things may be counterintuitive.

Impact of deprecation of third-party cookies

Ad-tech forms a very large part of the ecosystem of media and data. Most of the media and data today have symbiotic relationships, where tracking and targeting a user are now restricted under GDPR, CCPA, and so on. The browser itself poses restrictions in many cases. Apple's Safari blocked third-party cookie tracking for all the right reasons sometime back in 2019. This movement is being adopted by Firefox and Chrome who are blocking third-party cookies in formats. It will come up with a complete block on third-party cookies by January 2022. This will change a lot of things for the ad-tech world. This will also bring about a change in the previous user tracking methodologies. The new adaptations are supposed to make it easier for advertisers to target demographics, without hunting down specific users to ensure that the infrastructure used by many sites for logins does not break. In this way, advertisers will also get to know whether their advertisements are being converted into sales. This new method will open up an entirely new avenue for how ad tracking and privacy will work on the internet.

Regulations in the legal framework and tech formats will unequivocally change the way ad-tech systems work.

There will be two major things that will happen:

1. The anchor cookie will disappear. This means that no cross-origin scripts will get fired, and the publisher will have 100% control over all the cookies and data that gets collected. This also means that the publisher will have no choice but to take ownership of the controller.

2. Assuming the third-party paradigm is done with and the audience plays, it will shift to first-party data and the ad-serving will happen via second-party cookies. Most of the problems of data activation and user consent will get resolved.

Conclusion

Cookie mechanics is an important aspect of the ad-tech ecosystem. A cookie is required to track profiles and serve ads to the user. Deprecation of the cross-domain cookie means that a lot of things will change in terms of business alignment, data pathways, and media supply path. The next chapter talks about different data strategies and AI strategies.

Questions

1. What are the ways to drop a cookie?

2. What changes will be brought about in case of deprecation of third-party cookies?

Solutions

1. There are two ways to set a cookie:

    a. Via JS, where a JS can set a first-party cookie and also set a cross-domain cookie

    b. Via API, the admin can set a first-party cookie

2. Deprecation of third-party cookies on Google Chrome is a step by Google in direction of user privacy. However, the ad-tech industry looks at it as a monopolistic heavy-handedness that would allow Google to ascertain its dominance. Some of the implications of this move are as follows:

    a. DSP, SSP, and publisher, in today's format of working, may not be able to stay in sync.

    b. A site owner will have tighter control on services that would drop cookies.

    c. Many DMP player will go out of business.

CHAPTER 2
Data and AI Strategies

Introduction

Understanding data sources and creating a strategy become an important part of the DMP or CDP strategy. This chapter explains various data sources that are required in media buy and sell and the strategies that should be looked into for buy and sell intelligence.

Understanding the various data points, their features, and the AI/ML implications helps in a focused approach in implementing CDP/DMP and buy/sell strategies.

This chapter entails the various data universes, data sources, their attributes, AI/ML implementations, and roadmap that a brand and/or publisher can take grounds up. This is a vital aspect of any data-driven approach and should not be skipped.

Structure

- Different types of data sources:
  - RTB stream
  - Auction logs
  - Third-party data

- o   Personal identifiable Information

- o   Events

- o   Behavioral, deterministic, and intend data

- Types of data strategies

- Feature engineering to formulate a strategy

- AI- and ML-driven goals

- Thinking the audience

Objective

In ad-tech, data play is mandatory for all serious media buyers or sellers. Every data play consists of a data repository, strategies, and goals. Here, data is a very generic term, and ad-tech has a set of data that can be readily referred to.

In AI-driven objectives, data strategy has to be carefully formulated to manage the scale and density of the data in parallel. This becomes important and tricky because a data-driven design is hard to validate, and the results are almost impossible to troubleshoot.

A CDP undertaking has to start with clear business objectives in mind. A good data and AI strategy is a must for a CDP to give any meaningful result. As a CDP will usually work with a data-driven architecture, the selection of data sources, AI layer, and activation channels is very important.

Note: A CDP needs a good data strategy to succeed. One of the primary requirements in CDP is the AI component. For example, if the CDP has to work toward click optimization, then it will need a certain set of data to work with. CDP and DMP have certain commonality. However, the differences are really stiff. DMP essentially is used for data activation and basic segmentation. A CDP, on the other hand, can do these and is more focused on a business KPI. In the ad-tech, a CDP should focus on buy- or sell-side use cases. We will discuss the differences between CDP and DMP in the later chapters.

Different types of data sources

There are some standard data sources available in the programmatic ecosystem. The ecosystem itself is divided into the buy and sell side. The two commodities to trade are media and audience. The two primary methods to trade the commodities are syncs and RTB. Please note that the media also gets traded via S2S, tag, direct, and so on. From a media trading perspective, RTB can achieve all the features provided by S2S and tag and so on, but in this book, we will stick to programmatic. Also, the data is synced via S2S and offline methods, which I have not covered because that can become much customized in nature and vary hugely. Essentially, it is a server-to-server call to give out data; this may also be achieved via FTP dumps.

Note: A lot of DMPs have given out data to DSPs via dump till today.

RTB stream

The RTB protocol is used to communicate bid requests and its responses between sell and buy systems, respectively, in the ad-tech ecosystem. We will discuss the working of the RTB protocol in the later chapters. An RTB stream data is usually used by bidders for various optimization techniques. The RTB stream data gives a lot of inferences; some of them are as follows:

- It can tell all the publisher pages what the user has been going through. This is usually used to profile users.

- It can tell at what prices the bidder is winning the bids and at what prices the bidder is leaving the bids.

- The RTB stream represents the complete media universe. Using this universe for creating lookalikes and so on gives the best results.

- Some advanced teams have been able to derive over 80,000 dimensions. This makes it very potent to give data density for the AI layers.

The RTB data universe is also used by many DSPs as a media planning source. This also means that if all the DSPs use the same supply sources, then there is probably no need for independent media planning tools.

Note: Some DMPs also give lookalike features. DMPs do not have media coverage. They always have to deal with data activation where the next challenge comes with the match rates. As there are leakages between getting the reference base, creating lookalikes, and activation, the process cannot get into an iterative mode, which is usually required for KPIs. This is the reason why DMP-based lookalikes seldom work in a programmatic buy.

As the RTB stream constitutes the data based on the RTB protocol, the actual data collected is also based on the RTB protocol in use. The latest RTB version 2.5 seems to have gained popularity in the last few years. However, RTB also has 2.3 and 2.4 versions in existence.

Note: From legal data ownership perspective, the RTB stream data ownership can be attained by owning the bidder and the supply agreements.

You can find a comparative list of attributes used by the different versions of RTB in Annexure 1.

Looking at RTB, one begins to wonder why a programmatic ecosystem uses a parallel mechanism for data. In other words, why cannot the RTB stream itself be used for data? I think that if there were a way for data owners to monetize data within RTB, then the ecosystem can do without a separate stream for data sync and so on. This will help break the monopoly of the data, but there are many things that need to fall in place for this to happen.

> **Note: The details of that can be found at https://www.iab.com/wp-content/uploads/2016/03/OpenRTB-API-Specification-Version-2-5-FINAL.pdf.**

Auction logs

Auctions are conducted at exchange. This has another layer when talking about header-bidding systems. To keep things simple, let us stick to straightforward exchange systems for now. By the traditional definition, bidding and auction go hand-in-hand, and it is no different in the ad-tech world as well. Exchange generates bid requests for the bidder/DSP, and once it receives the bid response, which is usually from multiple DSPs/bidders, it conducts auctions. Essentially, at this point, the exchange has RTB stream data, bid response data from various bidders/DSPs, and the win decision data. This makes the exchange, the single source where all the control flows interject. Exchanges deploy first- and second-price auctions, but we will discuss that in the later chapters. A brief of what we can do with the auction data is as follows:

- We can know at what price the media has been sold. This is one out of the two biggest transparency issues in the programmatic ecosystem, as this data is always kept hidden from marketers and publishers.

- We can know all the advertisers who are bidding for the data. This data is necessary to build any model around price prediction. This is the other out of the two biggest transparency issues in the programmatic ecosystem.

- Auction data is the best form of data to figure out media frauds because we can find out all the bot and outlier traffic.

- Beyond this auction, data has all the features of the bid stream and an aggregated bid response. Please find the attributes for the bid request in Annexure 1 that has been attached at the end of this book.

> **Note: All of the marketer, agency, and DSP get the price point at which they have bought the inventory, but this usually includes all the margins that are built in the value chain. The same problem is with the publishers also. Since 2019, most of the bigger exchanges have support first-price auction. Theoretically, first-price auction is publisher friendly.**

Third-party data

It is typically the attributes that are provided by third-party data sources. For example, a user (u) is tracked within the publisher (pa), publisher (pb), and an advertiser (a). Publisher (pa) allocates segment (sa), publisher (pb) allocates segment (sb), and advertiser allocates segment(saa) to this user. For advertiser (a), segments (saa) is the first-party data, and (sa) and (sb) is the third-party data. This has been explained in detail in *Chapter 3 Working of DMP and CDP*. Third- and second-party data helps to build data density. This can be further used by AI as a dimension and/or filter in the bidder/DSP for campaign targeting.

Personal identifiable information

Personal Identifiable Information (PII). It is never used directly by any ad-tech platforms but used as a reference segment to create lookalikes. In such cases, we typically want to map the users with a cookie, device ID, or advertiser ID with the PII and then create a lookalike segment using the data universe. This will be covered in the later chapters.

> Note: The security and handling of PII are the central premise of GDPR and other upcoming regulations. It goes on to the other IDs that can be linked to the PII. Systems can break this link to make the data anonymous and continue to use the trends as learning.

Events

Events are usually triggered by the user. These are usually designed by the product owner to understand user behavior. At times, these events can be used in ad-tech systems as deterministic data. Most of the performance KPI are driven by them. The following is a sample **Amount Deposit** event – a sample set of data collected in an event can look as follows:

Parameter	Desc	Data type	Mandatory	Possible values
id	UniqueId	String	Yes	222
gamecategory	Category of game	String	Yes	championship
gametype	Type of game	String	Yes	gambling
gamesubtype	Sub-category of game	String	Yes	dice

amount	The amount deposited by the user to play game	String	Yes	5
devicetype	Type of device	String	No	IDFA or GAID, in case of the Web request, this value will be blank

Table 2.1: Sample attributes to capture an event

Events can be of multiple types. The data capture techniques can vary depending on the case. This will be covered later in the chapter.

Tip: Do not bother about the currency parameter; the app was only in one country.

Behavioral, deterministic, and intend data

Over some time, I have begun to formulate thumb rules to follow for every data play. For starters, the data source has to be placed in these deterministic, behavioral, and intend categories. A data repository should have a certain percentage of these data categories. They are as follows:

- There has to be about 0.1–1% deterministic data. Deterministic data is typically CRM data, PII, conversion data, and so on, that is 100% verifiable.

- There has to be about 2–7% behavioral data. Behavioral data is concluded signals, for example, clicks, visit on a page, and so on. This data is typically inferred by some activity done by the users. Usually, deterministic and behavioral signals are used in segmentation.

- The rest of it has to be intended data. Intend data is typically the universe, for example, RTB logs or auction data. The universe would have a lot of signals that are typically in raw format. A regular set of hierarchy may not be able to cover the whole universe.

Note: A lot of classification models use 2–7% of reference dataset to give usable results. Secondly, these can change depending on the availability and use case.

These rules are very broad, and one has to find a way to narrow it down in terms of data availability and density. Data density is defined by the number of signals of media and audience that has been provided. This is one of the make-or-break factors for AI to work.

Audience-based attributes are dependent on the user and depict different attributes for the same media. Some of the audience-based attributes are browser, geo, and so on.

> **Note: A segment is usually defined by certain rules. These rules usually work on URL filters, text filters, or macho filters. A signal is the raw input before it was used to classify the user into a segment. In certain lingo, it is also used as the segment itself. Some DMPs consider a user profile only when they have 20 attributes or more attached to it.**

Media-based attributes are more contextual and stay the same between all the users. They are content, Web/mobile-Web/app, site map, domain name, ad-unit, and so on.

The two critical time factors are relevance and freshness. Some DMPs also refer to them as recency and frequency. First of all, they are the age and strength of the signal, and secondly, for how much time those signals will be relevant. The strength of a signal can be defined by the number of times the signal has occurred in a selected time, typically referred to as frequency. Data is also represented by segments and hierarchies, but we will take a look at them in the later chapters.

Types of data strategies

The two distinct strategies for ad-tech consist of buy and sell. Both of them have distinct goals and processes.

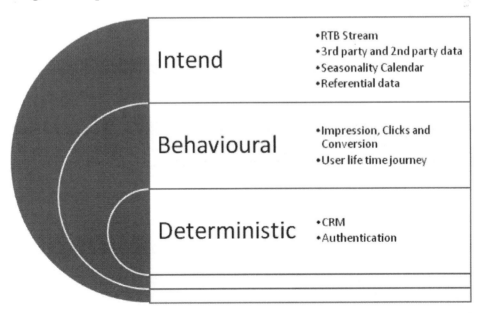

Figure 2.1: Segment Type vs Data Source

The buy-side of the ecosystem typically requires the following:

- Optimization for SPO, CPM, CPC, CPA, CPI, and so on.

- All other optimizations on lookalike and outlier support the earlier point.

- A lot of bidders/DSPs need to have some or all of these features in some or the other way.

This is where the difference between good and bad optimization can be seen. This is why some categories of buys do and do not work with certain platforms. Buy involves the understanding of the availability of media and audience, the opportunity identification in the bid request, and the ascertaining of the price bidder/DSP can afford to attain goals.

The sell side of the ecosystem is fairly complex and has to deal with the age-old problems of pricing and making the product attractive.

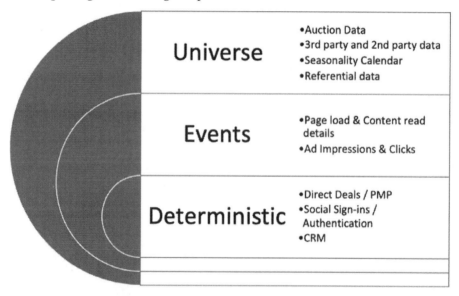

Figure 2.2: Segment type versus user/system-generated signals

- Dynamic floor pricing in RTB and the header-bidding system ensure the best price a seller can get in the auction.

- RTB enrichment for the supply enables the seller to get a better fill.

- Outlier media along with the audience needs to be pruned for the publisher to attain a quality of media.

Unfortunately, most of the sell systems do not have these features, and publishers are left at a chance to get their due share. So, in this case, it is usually about no system to some or good system.

Feature engineering to formulate a strategy

Once a good data strategy is in place, the next thing that needs to be done is a feature analysis exercise.

> **Note: Feature is a variable or attribute such as Geo, Publisher Name, and so on, and feature analysis is a process to figure out the features that can contribute to attaining the goal.**

Concepts like univariate and multivariate analysis are used to determine the efficacy of features. This is where the sample side of data begins to matter.

These analyses will go through the sample data and figure out if the feature changes are proportional or inversely proportional to the result. If there is no effect, then there is no need to consider the feature at all. The problem arises if the sample data is less and the analysis shows that the feature was not required, but in reality, the feature was important, and we just missed out on that.

Sample data is also used to test the models, so it is imperative to put adequate energy to make sure that the data strategy includes getting this data and updating it periodically.

AI- and ML-driven goals

Most of the goals today are AI/ML-driven in ad-tech. AI/ML is as good as the data it gets. A good data strategy and feedback loop make all the difference in the output of AI/ML.

I will not cover the detailed implementation of the AI technique but will try to help in understanding the underlying techniques and their relevance for the goals.

Let us start with a basic understanding of this. AI and ML can be broken down into a few broad categories:

- **Clustering**
    - It is essentially used to group the entities. Entities could be user, ad-unit, publisher, campaigns, and so on.
    - It does not require any labeled input data.
    - K-means algorithms
        - With the given data and defined number of clusters, an entity could be distributed into clusters. Entities are assigned to the clusters based on the nearest mean, that is, cluster center or centroid.
    - Distance metric

- Euclidean distance
- Cosine distance
- Jaccard distance

o Usually used for similar users, often known as lookalikes, similar media, and so on. Lookalikes, however, can go beyond the user.

- **Classification/regression**
  o In scenarios where we want to predict output based on historically labeled data, we use supervised ML models.

  o It usually requires user input, for example, click, install, bid wins.

  o Algorithms
    - Linear regression
      - As the word suggests, it uses historic data and plots it to predict future events.
      - Usually represents a trend with a straight line.
    - Logistic regression
      - For the classification-based models where the output label class is binary or multi-class.
      - The output is in the form of a probability score for each class.
    - Neural networks
      - In scenarios where we do not want to define a function and want the model to fit into its non-linear function based on defined architecture.
      - With more data, neural nets perform better.

  o Usually used for content recommendations such as CPA, CPI strategies, surge engine, and so on.

- **Natural Language Processing (NLP)**
  o At times, we need to deal with text-based content. NLP is used to extract features from the text.

  o NLP with neural nets is used to find inherited context from textual data.

  o It is used for similar content, similar users, content classification, and so on.

Goals dictate the usage of AI and the data strategy. Some of the buy-side goals are as follows:

- **Supply path optimization**
  - o In today's programmatic ecosystem, media can reach the bidder/DSP from multiple sources. Depending on which path the request has taken, the cost may differ. This generates a possibility of optimization.
  - o Essentially, we have to figure out the path, which is a sequence of exchanges on a publisher and/or ad-unit basis that has been fetching the least price.
  - o Algorithms: NLP and decision tree.
  - o Data source: RTB logs, impression logs, and win logs.

- **CPM – cost per mille**
  - o It essentially has two things that need consideration:
    - ▪ **Outlier**: If the media or audience is not up to the mark.
    - ▪ What is the least possible cost at which the inventory can be bought.
  - o CPM will always go for the highest probability block with the lowest price tag. This is in case the media or audience is not an outlier. The bidding range is usually attained by creating discrete price blocks, and the AL/ML chooses the best block to be used for the win.
  - o **Algorithm**: Classification-based neural net model.
  - o **Data source**: RTB logs, impression logs, and win logs.

- **CPC – cost per click**
  - o There are two things to be considered in CPC optimization:
    - ▪ The goal can ask the bidder to drop the cost to, say x, on a per click basis.
    - ▪ Secondly, the goal can ask the bidder to give, say y clicks, on a per-day basis.
  - o CPC scores the media and audience and uses a threshold to suggest if the request can fetch a win. Once this is done, the CPM algorithm takes over.
  - o **Algorithms**: Classification-based neural net model.
  - o **Data Source**: RTB logs, impression logs, and click logs.

- **CPA/CPI/CPS – performance**
  - o All the CPx works similarly. They can follow a simple goal of acquisition, install, and so on, or can go further by saying install and 2 activates in the next 7 days. In all cases, these are treated as events. The goals are in the lines of CPC.
    - ▪ A typical approach is as follows:
    - ▪ Scope media, an audience concerning the KPI.
  - o Take out the outliers and go for the win. At this point, the CPM algorithm takes over.
  - o **Algorithm**: Classification-based neural net and lookalike models.
  - o **Data source**: RTB stream, impression logs, click logs, CRM data, and event logs.

Note: The data availability and its density make all the difference in implementing the AI/ML. AI is a very creative field, and engineers and data scientists constantly find new and better ways to do things at a very rapid pace. A good bidder needs to be able to incorporate the AI models at a rapid rate.

Most of the DSPs have favorites and may use different techniques for media buy.

The selling part has unfortunately been neglected for a long time, and the situation continues to be so. It has two primary goals:

- **Surge – Dynamic floor price-based optimization**
  - o A surge mechanism enables the publisher to provide dynamic pricing in the originating bid request.
  - o **Algorithm**: Linear regression, logistic regression.
  - o **Data source**: Auction data, second- and third-party data, CRM data, seasonality calendar, clicks, social sign-ins, and so on.
- **Enrichment – Populating RTB parameters**
  - o RTB has over 200 parameters. Enrichment attempts to populate a maximum number of fields.
  - o This is targeted toward the campaign so that they can qualify.
  - o **Algorithm**: NLP.
  - o **Data source**: Content, second- and third-party data, CRM data, click, content read by the user, and so on.

Note: Many companies, including top 3 SSPs, do not use AI from the publisher side to enhance eCPM. Hence, this becomes a very new thing for them. It only makes sense because the advertiser is paying for the complete technology stack, so the entire tech is essentially playing in favor of the advertiser.

Thinking the audience first way

There are two schools of thought in the audience play. It starts by identifying the following:

- **Buy**: If you are the media and data buyer.
- **Seller**: If you are the media and/or data seller.

Usually, there is a clear divide between the two unless you are an e-commerce or similar kind of player who is an advertiser and publisher alike and hence a buyer and seller both.

Thinking business in terms of data typically means thinking about three angles that one needs to take care of. They are as follows:

- Usually, data can be in-housed along with some part of the activation channel that can be in-housed.

- Regulations surrounding the business and data from a geo-market perspective.

- The market integrations that will be required to connect buying and selling of the media and data.

This gives us about 8 things to cover to complete the "audience first" thought process:

	Buy	**Sell**
Data	Go for a CDP if you want CRM to be a part of the buying process. This typically becomes evident if you want to use programmatic for user engagement.	Go for a CDP if you want CRM to be a part of the selling process. This typically becomes evident if you use CDP for user engagement via other channels.
	Use a DMP if a CRM is not part of your strategy.	You can use a DMP for direct demand execution and data activation to a certain extent.
	If you want to center the buy around your first-party data, then CDP/DMP in-housing becomes necessary.	In case you want to base your sell strategy on data, then you will be required to shift to first-party data, and CDP/DMP in-housing will become necessary.

Activation	If you want to have control over buy logic using media and data at the core level, then you will need to have an in-house bidder/DSP. In all cases, you will want to have tight control over the supply sources.	If you want to control eCPM, then you will need to have an in-house exchange or header bidding system. In all cases, you want to keep a tight control of on-demand sources.
Regulations	A marketer is a part controller, and for most parts, a processor depends on the dataset. In all cases, they have a consumer-facing front. Having a CDP/DMP stack that can withstand the new regulations that are cropping up and complex treatments of data that percolates to data strategy and data activation is a must.	A publisher is a pure controller and is subject to rather complicated regulatory scenarios. A publisher is becoming the gatekeeper of user consent. This makes at least one more system talking with the ad-tech stack that a publisher is deploying.
Integrations	A buyer needs to integrate data and media with the supplier who can ideally provide overlying media and data. In certain cases, the buyer would want to get the two from different parties that make extra requirements on attribution.	A supplier needs to connect with multiple buy systems. A seller will require a third-party DMP or preferably a second-party DMP for data trading. This is also useful to attract better eCPM.

Table 2.2: Strategic decisions around data

A typical in-housing journey would look like the following figure. The data is the first part, and AI operations do get impacted with the decisions that would need to be taken in the initial phases. Hence, the data strategy part becomes very critical for success.

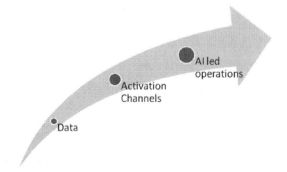

Figure 2.3: Shows in-housing data journey's milestones

The journey of in-housing can start from any operation or function of a business; however, a natural progression will start from setting up a DMP/CDP, then forming activation channels and the final setup of AI-led operations.

This not only gives a solid foundation but also a path for business continuity.

In the e-com scenario, where one has to adopt both the strategies, it becomes critical to understand things from the following aspects:

Buy and/or sell scenarios	Need to do
Generating traffic for the site as a regular marketer.	Buy media from external publishers.
Generating traffic for brands present in the e-commerce portfolio.	Prospecting users within an e-commerce portal or external publishers. Re-target users from external publishers.
Once the portal real estate is earmarked for marketing for brands then in a way the media is up for bidding.	Use the SSP-side bidding system for maximizing the media revenue.

Table 2.3: Use cases for media buy and sell and its tactical solution

This is the reason that e-commerce players usually deploy very advanced ad-tech stacks.

Conclusion

A CDP is usually a large and complex undertaking for any organization. A good data strategy can help in making it a successful one. The data strategy should consist of fixing the buy or sell goals, designing an underlying AI foundation, designing the activation channels and its interfaces with the CDP, and possibly conducting a dry run with AI layer and sample datasets from available data sources to see if all the goal aspects are being catered. Once the data strategy is clear, the CDP journey becomes the next natural step. The next chapter will cover the working of DMP and CDP and also how to put forth a blueprint if one wants to opt for in-housing.

Questions

1. Why is a good data strategy important?

2. Define a generic data strategy for an advertiser.

3. Define a generic data strategy for a publisher.

4. How do you create a checklist for CDP by undergoing the data strategy exercise?

Solutions

- **Answer 1**: A CDP, DSP, and exchange are tools and platforms that becomes sharper with data. A CDP in particular is a very configurable and dynamic platform. The AI layer provided by CDP needs data breadth and depth to perform the relevant task. A good data strategy keeps a view of the business end goal and aligns the data via appropriate purposing. A good data strategy is a make or break of any in-housing.

- **Answer 2**: An advertiser typically has brand or performance goals. In both scenarios, he/she is trying to get a better ROI or "bang for the buck." Typically, an advertiser should formulate the strategy around the media universe, impressions, clicks, conversions, and LTV-based events. Branding KPIs are more around reach and recall, whereas performance KPIs are more sales-focused and want to relate to sales figures.

- **Answer 3**: A publisher wants more fill and better eCPM of his/her inventory. A DSP, on the other end, does a lot of filtering for the incoming bids. A publisher should enrich media to get a better chance of clearing the DSP filters. The media of publisher that can clear the DSP filter has very high chance of getting bought.

- **Answer 4**: A checklist for a CDP is based on the business goals being set. A publisher's goal versus an advertiser's goals would be very different and hence would reflect on the CDP implementation. The following are the steps for creating the checklist:

    1. Set mid- to long-term business goals.
    2. Create data universe.
    3. Fix AI implementation.
    4. Design the relevant interfaces with the bidder and/or exchange or any other platform.

CHAPTER 3

Working of DMP and CDP

Introduction

This chapter should help in putting up a checklist to select a seat of **Customer Data Platform (CDP)** or **Data Management Platform (DMP)**. This could also help to put forth a blueprint for a CDP or DMP that you may want to be in-housed. This makes the CDP/DMP knowledge crucial for everyone in the programmatic ecosystem. I have tried to incorporate buy, sell, and data trading aspects in the chapter as well.

In a way, one might say that DMP is the predecessor of CDP. However, in today's time, DMP and CDP both are well established, and both are constantly changing. DMP is mostly a standard product and is used in data activation and related activities. A CDP has many flavors and integral features for advance buy, sell, and user engagement-based use cases.

Due to legacy issues with the ad-tech ecosystem where the RTB protocol is heavily underutilized for any kind of data sharing or data operations, the DMP and CDP play a very important role in ad-tech with the audience.

As most of the buyers and sellers want to have a data-first approach, a DMP or CDP or both become an important piece in the overall stack.

This chapter entails the working of DMPs and CDPs. This forms the "tools and technique" part of the data strategy. In the case of the data-first approach, this forms the first step.

Structure

- Defining DMPs and CDPs
- Use cases of ad-tech-focused DMPs and CDPs
- Data activation
- Buy-side ROI
- Sell-side monetization
- Engagement
- Data acquisition methodologies
- Hierarchies and segments
- Data transparency aspects
- The first-, second- and third-party data
- AI-generated segments
- Types of segments
- Attribution
- Overlaying data of different data sources
- Recommend Big Data-based architecture for an in-housed CDP
- Challenges of activating data

Objective

The reader is advised to understand the data strategy aspects before diving into any DMP and/or CDP text. Essentially, a data strategy is the planning phase of any CDP or DMP design and deployment. Of course, at times, one may need to understand the use cases before he/she can get into data strategy. But again, one cannot attain any CDP- or DMP-based goals before having the data strategy component in place.

With this chapter, you should be able to put up an execution plan to implement a CDP/DMP and have clarity on the goals and/or use cases that you want to target.

Defining DMPs and CDPs

Let us start with the basic concepts first and then understand the core requirement that they try to adhere to:

DMP

- A DMP is a software platform that is responsible for agglomeration of website data and categorizing it into taxonomies that are used in building segments.

- It hosts hierarchies along with some of its segments. In most cases, a CDP/DMP user can make his/her own private hierarchy that will only be visible to him/her. The public hierarchy is usually common for all the CDP/DMP users.

- A DMP is used for data activation between platforms, for example:

    o A DSP can use third-party data, via DMP, for prospecting.

    o A publisher can use third-party attributes for content personalization.

- A DMP usually does not host **Personal Identifiable Information (PII)**. This is due to its intrinsic design. If PII or its associate ID gets synced, then the DMP will have to track the user and comply with the data regulatory norms. Technically, this becomes an impossible task, and the DMP stays out of this liability.

- Sometimes, a DMP also provides features of lookalike and so on.

- DMPs usually work with only behavioral data. Hence, even segments like age may be probabilistic in nature.

- Usually, a DMP works with a third-party cookie as an anchor ID mechanism.

Note: Some DMPs, while contracting for the DMP/CDP seat, will ask not to host any PII.

CDP

- A **CDP** is a service that pulls data from multiple sources and combines it together to create a persistent unified customer database across multiple channels, technologies, and devices.

- A CDP also hosts hierarchies and segments.

- A CDP can also perform data activations between platforms on first-, second- and third-party data. This allows a CDP to work with **PII**.

- As a CDP can handle legal compliance and work with PII, it is apt to integrate with **Customer Relationship Management (CRM)** and use its dataset for any desired purpose.

- CDPs can work with large datasets of intent, behavioral, and deterministic signals.

- Some flavors for a CDP are:

  1. A CDP, on the one end, can be a replacement of a CRM and be very agnostic of activation channels.

  2. A CDP can focus on one kind of dataset and focus on activation and reporting.

  3. A CDP can focus on incorporating AI layers for attaining **Key Performance Indicators (KPIs)**.

It is easy to see that just a few things at the core level can make such a huge difference. This is where the underlying difference comes in:

CDP	DMP
It manages and works with PII.	It does not work with PII.
It can be used with tight integration to DSP and SSP.	It usually works independently.
Usually works with advanced and custom feature sets.	It works primarily with data activation.

Table 3.1: CDP versus DMP

> **Note: One can only look to in-house a CDP. Also, an in-housed CDP may require some channel for data activation if they choose to work with many DSPs and DMP. If your requirement is only data activation, then do not get into data in-housing of any format.**

I think that CDP has a targeted focus because of the way it has been designed for execution. Supposedly, you have arrived at data strategy and now want to use it for buy and/or sell; in that case, a CDP makes the good choice if the data strategy goes beyond data activation.

On the other hand, the new DMPs have been graduated to work with second-party data. This in a way solves a lot of problems of data transparency by design. However, I must say that not a lot of DMPs have a rounded feature set to manage second-party data trading. With the knowledge of ID mechanics, cookie syncs, and data strategy, you would be ready to dive into the world of CDP.

> **Note: You can find the IAB data transparency standards at: https://iabtechlab. com/wp-content/uploads/2019/06/Data-Transparency-Standard-1.0-Final-June-2019.pdf.**

Use cases of ad-tech-focused DMPs and CDPs

There are many use cases of DMPs and CDPs. They can be classified into the following:

- **Data activation**: It is acquiring user data from one platform to another.
- **Buy-side ROI**: Attaining return on investments, typically media buy budgets, to drive effective business goals.
- **Sell-side monetization**: Driving revenue by selling media.
- **Engagement**: It includes increasing traffic based on user preference by putting up relevant content, product, and so on.
- **Consumer insights**: Understanding user behavior with the help of various analyses.
- **Media planning**: A set of insights that helps the trader to plan media for buy or sell strategies.

Note: CDP institute's checklist can give a wide range of things that a CDP can do. However, it is a more generic explanation. One needs to derive use cases on the basis of industry. CDPs are also used in mar-tech where the systems deal with SMS and e-mail marketing. Although consumer insights do require all the data from all the channels, which is also the usual case, but for now, we will leave that out from the scope of this book.

PS: CDPs can also be used for other CRM activities and can choose to complete with them. The list can vary depending on the industry.

Data activation

From the data activation perspective, a DMP and CDP play a similar role where the data gets synced between various platforms. *Figure 3.1* gives the details of the entities where the CDP/DMPs usually sync the data. Also, note that these entities are very similar to the ID syncs that we had discussed in the earlier chapters.

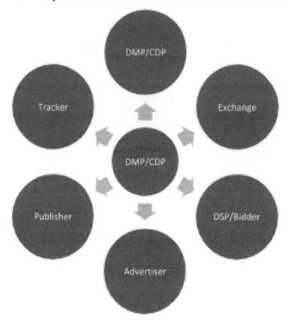

Figure 3.1: CDP Business use case

The process usually consists of two phases:

- **ID syncs**: Some platforms also refer to them as ID-swaps.

    1. This is usually a real-time process in case of cookies.

    2. In the case of device ID or advertiser ID, this step is not required.

- **Data transfers**: This is where the user Id -> segment map is transferred between the entities.

    1. The data transfers are done in real time and offline mode.

    2. Depending on the data provider and the regulatory restrictions, the data segment may be limited.

Buy-side ROI

A marketer's key responsibility, like any other buyers, is to derive the maximum return on investments of the marketing budget.

An advanced ad-tech buy-focused CDP is also capable of transferring the buy-centric AI model definition to be used by the activation channel. This would appear as follows:

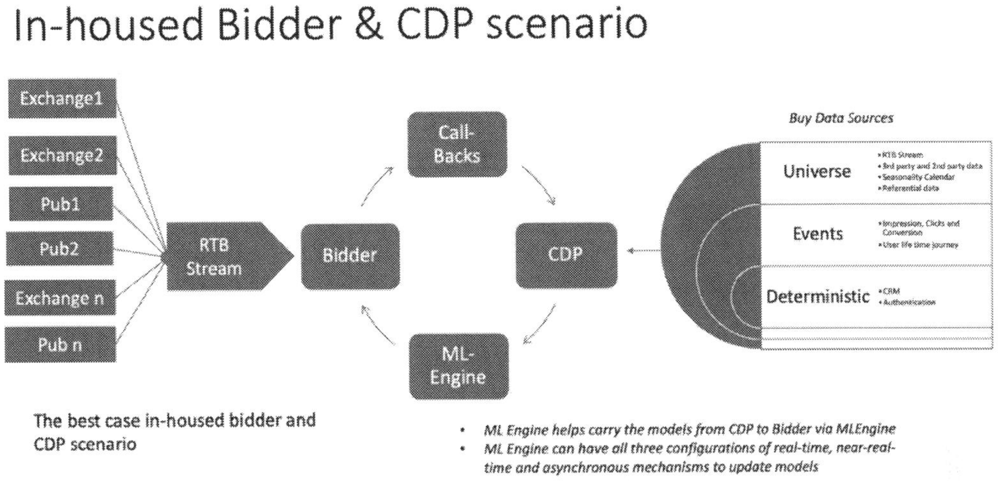

In-housed Bidder & CDP scenario

The best case in-housed bidder and
CDP scenario

- *ML Engine helps carry the models from CDP to Bidder via MLEngine*
- *ML Engine can have all three configurations of real-time, near-real-
  time and asynchronous mechanisms to update models*

***Figure 3.2**: High-level view of CDP working with a bidder*

This scenario assumes a lot of components and integrations, which are as follows:

- The CDP supports AI layers consisting of buy algorithms such as SPO, CPM, CPC, CPI, CPA, and so on.

- This AI layer is an ML engine that creates and updates the models.

- These models are integrated with the bidder, and the campaigns in the bidder are able to use them.

Note: This is a greenfield scenario. A typical brownfield scenario will be much more complex because it will have multiple CDPs, bidders, and perhaps, inadequate data source. Nevertheless, an in-housed CDP should be flexible enough to accommodate all these factors in its design. The AI-driven working of the goals and the working of bidder itself are explained in detail in the bidder section of the later chapters.

Sell-side monetization

One of the key responsibilities of the media seller is to attain revenues at a consistently high rate. This is done by managing and balancing the inventory price and fill rates. For this, a CDP is used by the publishers to optimize **the Effective Cost Per Mile (eCPM)**. This tackles the age-old problem of media and audience pricing. In the case of RTB, this is done in a high-frequency mode, and the pricing gets set rather quickly.

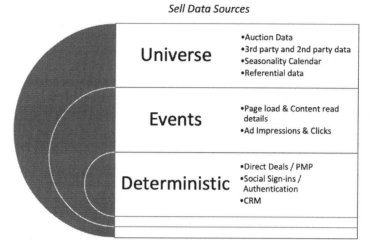

Figure 3.3: *Segment type vs Data Source*

In *Figure 3.3*, the content can constitute a range of digital products. For example, books, tickets, subscription plans, and so on. Also, the content and audience could have different behaviors even within the same company group sites. Hence, this becomes a rather generic categorization of the data source, and one has to understand the content to formulate a good sell-side data strategy.

An in-housed sell-side system would look as follows:

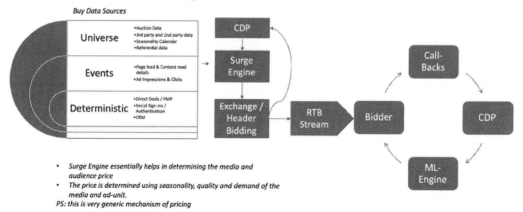

Figure 3.4: *High-level view of CDP working with exchange/SSP*

In essence, the CDP tries to give intelligence to the exchange to set up the floor price in the most adequate way. In other words, it helps exchange to maximize the yield.

Note: The AI-driven working of the goals, the working of exchange, and the header bidding system are explained in detail in the later chapters. An optimal yield works between two variables of fill and eCPM, which are very dynamic in nature. It is like setting up a price in the demand–supply curve for a product. For an exceptional case like this one, the price needs to be optimized on every transaction for the optimal results. The exchange conducts auction between the DSPs using the floor price that the publisher has set.

Engagement

A publisher may choose to deploy multiple channels to keep a user engaged. For many business reasons, the mechanism could entail the following goals:

- A user may stay on a page for longer, for example, reads the entire article, reviews a product, and so on.

- A user has new and relevant content, that is, freshness and relevant factors.

- A user has followed-up content.

- A user has surveys to participate in.

This is a broad idea of how a publisher would be thinking; the content type may define the actual implementation.

Note: Feature extraction is a means to extract context from content. The context representation and content's inherent complexity adds to the complexity of the feature extraction. This is the reason why feature extraction becomes very complex and critical while working with different content types. Further to this, the features that are extracted are used as inputs to the AI/ML algorithms, and hence, skipping this process is not really an option.

At this point, we also need to define different perspectives of engagement for a different type of publishers. They are as follows:

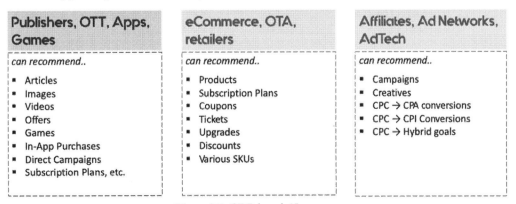

Figure 3.5: CDP-based AI use cases

Please note the CPC -> CPA conversion is being depicted as the recommendation mechanism. From the bidder perspective, it loses control of the flow post the moment a user has clicked on the ad-banner/video and so on. However, CPA-based algorithms go beyond this scope and use acquisition data from CRM and figure out similar media and audience from the universe. This is explained in the later chapters.

A typical recommendation system deployed by a publisher would look like as depicted in *Figure 3.6.*

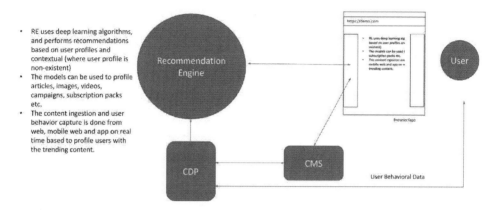

Figure 3.6: *High-level view of a CDP-driven recommendation system with text content*

Although a recommendation system does not come under programmatic, but if we talk about deriving performance from programmatic, such systems do become an add-on to the ad-tech stack itself.

Note: A publisher can choose to deploy a single CDP that can back both user engagement and monetization goals.

Data acquisition methodologies

One of the critical steps in any CDP or DMP process is data acquisition. Data can be represented as signals coming in via event variables that are assigned some context. These contexts are further used to create segments.

There are primarily two kinds of data acquisition methods:

1. Real time
2. Offline

The real-time method typically consists of getting data over the "http or https" protocol, messaging queue system, or socket. This method allows for bi-directional communication. Depending on the methodology being used, the system can attain the following features:

1. **Http/https**: It is a session-based protocol. It is usually initiated from the browser client. It is also used for server-to-server (system to system) communication. This protocol works on top of TCP/IP.

2. **Messaging queue**: It is based on the producer–consumer framework, and it is usually used for server to server communication. There is no session involved, as this messaging system delivers high throughput of messages. This mechanism works on top of TCP/IP.

3. **Socket**: It can be defined by the IP address plus port. It works in the client–server mode. Socket-based communication can be based on UDP and TCP both. UDP is used for a closed network and can deliver throughput of 2x that of TCP. This method can get very high throughputs.

In ad-tech, most of the real-time communication happens over "http/https." Hence, we will not get into the working of messaging and socket-based communication over here. There are two primary methods of http/https:

1. **Get**: The get parameter supports the passing of parameters in the URL itself. In general, the URL length should be under 2,000 characters. There is no rule as such, but some browsers have their limitations, and we need to take cognizance of this because we do not want to miss out on any data calls. Some find this as a security issue because the browser may show all the parameters that one may be passing.

    For example:

    ```
    ?id=123,deviceid=xyz,devicetype=idfa/gaid,emailed=v@abc.com,attribute=2017-07-24,phone=9820945596,src=campaignname
    ```

2. **Post**: It is similar to the get request, except it passes all the data via the message body. In general, a post is considered to be secure and is able to send much larger chunks of data.

    For example:

    ```
    → API Endpoint :
    production
    https://sample.app.com/event/register
    → Sample Input Json(body) :
    {
        "id" : "123",
        "deviceid":"xyz",
    ```

```
"devicetype":"idfa/gaid",
"emailed":"v@abc.com",
"attribute" : "2017-07-24",
"phone" : 961xxxxx73,
"src" : "campaignname"
        }
```

From data collection and disbursal standpoint, there are two ways to look at it:

1. In a scenario where a user site sends data to a server (DMP/CDP) and the CDP/DMP acknowledges the receipt of the data. This is a fairly straightforward way to handle in and out of data in the client–server mode or server-to-server mode. This is specifically used in getting a conversion, event, and so on type of data.

2. In a scenario such as ID sync, click tracking, and so on, an http/https redirect happens. Essentially, these kinds of scenarios happen when the flow needs to touch base with an interim system to collect some pieces of data before the control reaches the end goal.

   For example, the pixel piggybacking, which entails cookie drops, all cookies have to be in sync if multiple systems are done using this redirect.

The details of cookie sync have been explained in the earlier chapters.

Note: Http and https are basically the same protocol, except https uses an SSL certificate to encrypt the communication, whereas http is not secure and is susceptible to man-in-the-middle attachment data leak and so on. Https is secure, and except the domain name, everything in the body and header is encrypted.

The offline communication typically consists of dumping of csv, xls, and so on files to a predefined location. This is usually an FTP/FTPS server or S3 buckets. The recipient typically would run an hourly or daily (some time period) job to fetch the files and process them. One case where this is used very commonly is to transfer the audience data from one system to another (DMP -> DSP). Usually, post the ID sync, the sender would send the user segment details using the relevant ID. This mechanism can be used to transfer massive amounts of data in one go.

Hierarchies and segments

If data sync and transfer are the veins of a system, then hierarchies and segments are the heart and blood of this system (DMP and CDP). In simpler terms, hierarchies and segments are used to group audiences and provide context between audience groups. In addition to this, once you have the various mixes of data defined in the data strategies, one just needs hierarchies and segments to put the data in a usable format by DMP/CDP, bidder, exchange, and other systems.

A segment is a group of users that share certain behavior or attributes. For example, User1 and User could be between the age of 18 and 25 years. User1 could be an "intended traveler" because he has been visiting travel websites. This can be viewed in *Figure 3.7*:

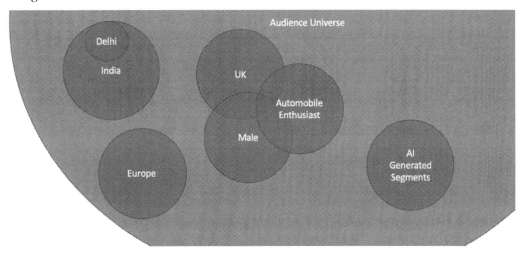

Figure 3.7: *Segment and data universe*

When assigning segments to the user, primarily, two things happen:

- **Case 1**: User to segment map

  o   User1 -> [seg1, seg2, seg3]

  o   User2 -> [seg1, seg3, seg5]

  o   User3 -> [seg6]

- **Case 2**: Segment to user map

  o   Seg1: [User1, User2]

  o   Seg2: [User1]

  o   Seg3: [User1, User2]

  o   Seg5: [User2]

  o   Seg6: [User3]

Assignment of segments to the user is determined by the signal. Anyways, user segmentation has been going on for multiple decades, but audience plays in programmatic happened post-2013. Again, from this book's perspective, we will stick to programmatic and will not cater to segments played in a non-programmatic world.

> **Note: Segments can become very intrusive in nature and can get into the realm of identity politics paradigm. On the other hand, larger DMPs today can have over 5,000 segments. Segments are required to make the audience usable by DMP, CDP, bidder, and exchange. Without segmentation, the audience play simply does not work.**

A hierarchy is defined as a multi-level index of segments. Now say, for example, a CDP has 5,000 segments; hence, this will make any human navigation within segments for any type of targeting impossible. It is the same as finding a home without a navigation map of the city. To find a segment, an operator needs to have a context, and the segments need to be linked with the context. In other words, all segments need to be indexed in a way that an operator can find the most relevant segment. This can be shown with a few examples, as shown in *Figure 3.8*, which depicts a geography-based hierarchy.

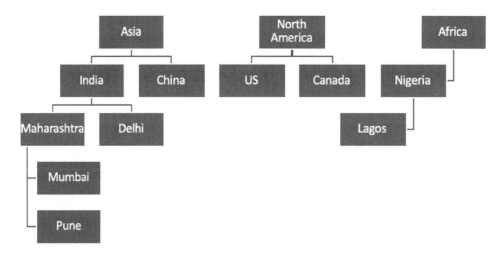

Figure 3.8: Sample Hierarchy

The geo-hierarchy is usually the simplest one among the others. A more complex set of the hierarchy is composed of brand and products. *Figure 3.9* tries to depict a circular relationship one may come across:

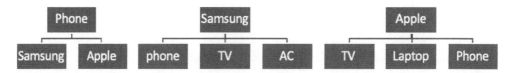

Figure 3.9: Sample Hierarchy

These kinds of complex relationships can become fairly complex in structuring data. When the probability of user tones down to belonging to multiple segments and one segment can belong to multiple hierarchies, further complexities come in due to data ownership and first-, second-, and third-party data paradigm. Let us break this down further in continuance to our Case 2:

- **Case 3**: Single owner scenario
    - **Hierarchy1**: [seg1 -> seg2, seg2 -> seg3, seg2 -> seg5]
    - **Hierarchy2**: [seg1 -> seg5]

From a marketers' or publishers' perspective, when they get a CDP/DMP account/ seat, they get a set of hierarchies and data along with it. This is usually public in nature. This means that all the entities (marketer and publisher) get a seat and will be able to view this data. This is also one of the primary offerings of a DMP, which is represented by several users and segments. An advanced buyer of CDP/DMP seats may also ask for the number of hierarchies, segments, and audience. From the marketers' and publishers' perspective, this becomes third-party data. However, a marketer and/or a publisher can host their own hierarchies and segment; this becomes first-party data. Let us process with Case 4 where Brand1 has not gotten a seat and hosting hierarchies and segments.

- **Case 4**: With public and Brand1 hosting first-party data
    - **Hierarchy3{owner Brand1}**: [seg31 -> seg32]
    - **Seg31{owner Brand1}**: [User1,User2]
    - **Seg32{owner Brand1}**: [User3]
    - **User3 :** [owner Brand1.Seg32, DMP/CDP.Seg6]

Please note that User3 was also assigned Seg6 in Case 1. This means that a user was found in two segments belonging to two different owners, which becomes a brand to the DMP/CDP relationship. This is first-party data to third-party data scenario. This is a common scenario in the DMP world when a user is found within multiple segments and the segment belongs to various hierarchies with different owners.

> **Note: Hierarchies make segments readable for humans. Beyond a certain threshold, navigating segments without a hierarchy is humanly impossible. Imagine a DSP operator checking 20,000 segments one-by-one for setting up targeting for a campaign. Phew! I hope you get the idea.**

Data transparency aspects

In the world of programmatic, data is extensively used and sometimes abused. Furthermore, data attribution has always been a challenge. This somewhat translates that data owners find it extremely hard to sell data in any context. The advent of GDPR and other regulations have made certain parts of this simpler by providing clarity on the responsibilities of the various stakeholders. However, this does not mean that things have eased down.

IAB has also released a data transparency standard. While we will cover a lot of that in our text from a programmatic context, covering the IAB standard is out of scope.

Data transparency percolates down to giving clarity about ownership and terms of data usage, the definition of segments and quantification of quality parameters. As a data source is a set of segments, one may argue that such parameters can be defined at the data source level. However, most of the CDP/DMP would host data of multiple owners, and hence, it becomes imperative that such quantification and identification mechanisms can be placed at the segment level. Some of the parameters that can help detail out a segment are as follows:

1. **Segment name**: Name of the segment.

2. **Owner name**: Company/entity name who owns the segment data.

3. **Owner contact information**: E-mail ID, phone, and so on, where the owner can be contacted.

4. **Criteria**: The definition of the segment. For example, a loyal user segment for a publisher can mean that a user visits the publisher's site at least 12 times in 30 days.

5. **ID type**: Anchor ID of the said segment with which the segment data can be accessed. For example, publisher, a cookie ID, e-mail, and so on.

6. **Geography**: Coverage of the geographical location for the audience set.

7. **Policy**: The policy link or text that governs the privacy policy of the segment.

8. **Source**: The source of data, for example, Web usage, app usage, clicks, signal, and so on.

9. Type: This helps in identifying the segment essence of data, for example, inferred, deterministic, declared, lookalike, outlier, and so on.

10. **ID maps**: Other entities with which the segment is getting synced.

11. **Freshness**: How frequently the data is getting refreshed, that is, real time, hourly, daily, monthly, yearly, or static.

12. **Relevance window**: In certain segments, the time period of the segment data matters. For example, sale of the product has to be defined by some time period, that is, daily, weekly, monthly, and so on.

Note: Segment definition is an important aspect of holding segments. This kind of annotation to a segment helps in regulatory compliance, attribution, targeting, quality check, and so on. Most of the CDP/DMPs do not follow this kind of a structure. In my view, this is just lazy design and any mistake that can become very costly.

The first-, second-, and third-party data

This is a relative paradigm of ownership of data. From a CDP/DMP perspective, this is limited to the access and ownership of data/segments.

Note: First-, second- and third-party data does not pertain to hierarchy as such. This is simply because the hierarchy may be a map, but segment is the actual dataset.

This will be a bit easier to explain with an example:

Seg7{owner Brand1}:[User1,User2]

Seg8{owner Brand2}:[User2, User 3]

Seg9{owner DMP/CDP}: [User1, User2, User3]

Seg10{owner DMP/CDP}: [User2]

Usually, the CDP/DMP has a report called the **audience profile report**. This usually caters to all the first- and third-party attributes that a user has.

As Brand1, I would see the data as:

- **User1**: {owner Brand1}.seg7, {owner DMP/CDP}.seg9
- **User2**: {owner Brand1}.seg7, {owner DMP/CDP}.seg9, {owner DMP/CDP}. seg10

From Brand1's perspective, Seg9 and Seg10 are third-party data.

As Brand2, I would see the data as:

- **User2**: {owner Brand2}.seg8, {owner DMP/CDP}.seg9, {owner DMP/CDP}. seg10
- **User3**: {owner Brand2}.seg8, {owner DMP/CDP}.seg10

From Brand2's perspective, seg9 and seg10 are third-party data.

In case, Brand1 and Brand2 want to drop each other's cookies in their respective domains, then they will be able to share data as stated earlier. The sync process is explained in the earlier part of the chapter. This is a second-party data scenario.

As Brand 1, I would see segments of Brand2:

- **User2**: {owner Brand1}.seg7, {owner Brand2}.seg8

And as Brand 2, I would see segments of Brand 1:

- **User2**: {owner Brand2}.seg8, {owner Brand1}.seg7

As you can see, that in second-party data, both sides may end up with the identical copy of data. The only difference will be visible in the activation part. This will be described in the latter part of the chapter. The activation decides the usage of the data in ad-serving.

> **Note: The second-party data mechanism is primarily used to share data on a one-to-one basis between advertisers to publishers or advertiser to advertisers or publishers to publishers. In the near future, this perhaps would be only way to trade data.**

AI-generated segments

There are various methodologies for creating AI/ML-based segments. It is based on the signals generated by different origins, for example, articles read, images seen, clicks, conversions, product purchased, and the relevant data universe; AI/ML algorithms can create lookalikes and outlier segments.

A high-level process to create a lookalike may be as follows:

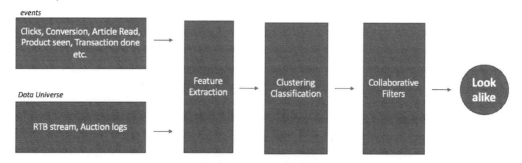

Figure 3.10: Flow of a lookalike model

A general process may look as follows:

1. We create a reference segment using event data. This is a subset of the data universe.

2. We extract features of the users' reference base.

3. We use one of the algorithms such as a neural network, k-means, and so on to form behavioral matrices.

4. We use collaborative filters to reduce multiple matrices to one user group.

A lookalike user base is used to derive performance and prospecting purposes. This kind of audience segmentation, once done properly, can be multi-folded better than any rule-based segment for prospecting or performance.

Outliers can be found in the media and audience. The media or the audience consists of the ones that do not work for a certain campaign, goal, category, or the entire buy or sell cycle. Usually, such audience segments are blacklisted at campaign, bidder, or exchange level.

This can include spoofed domain, bot users, spoofed IP-based originated users, and so on. A high-level view of finding outliers can be as follows:

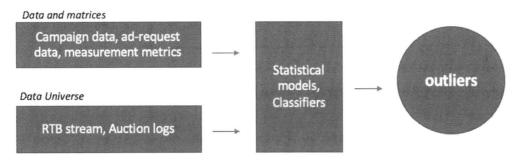

Figure 3.11: *Flow for an outlier*

Usually, statistical models and classifiers are used to identify the segments that do not work and should be pruned.

Lookalike and outlier audience segments play a very important part. Also, it is important to be aware of the reference segments that they are using. From the data perspective, it would be as follows:

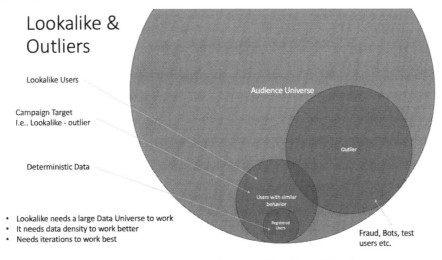

Figure 3.12: *Segments, data universe, and its AI manifestations*

At this point, it is important to understand that a lookalike will aim to represent the context of the reference segment.

Note: There can also be similar media and outlier media. But, that goes beyond the CDP/DMP context. We will cover this topic in the later chapters. Lookalikes are also referred as similar users by many platforms and professionals.

Types of segments

There are many schools of thought to create a definition of a segment. They cater to various degrees of context, relevance, freshness, and seasonality. From a buy-side CDP perspective, a CDP can store segments of media and audience both. From a sell-side CDP perspective, we can create segments of advertisers and campaigns. In this chapter, I am trying to provide a foundation as to how segmentation can be done without making it overly complicated and hence have left out advanced cases from the text. In most cases, the context of the media is percolated down to the audience. In case the audience data is unavailable, the media context is used. In most cases, this becomes a block buy. In most cases, media-based segments become out of scope for CDP/DMPs.

Types of segments are as follows:

1. **Psychometric segments**: These are derived on the premise of a psychological construct of the person. This construct also encompasses brands, products, media, and general behaviors. These are generally offline segments and cannot be used in programmatic. This is usually used to represent offline surveys and so on.

2. **RFM-based segments**: Recency, frequency- and monetary-based segments are typically used to understand the loyalty and value grade of the user. This is heavily used by retailers, B2C companies, travel, and so on, everywhere the marketer or publisher has to do targeting based on loyalty and/or product price tag.

   a. **Recency**: This typically suggests the freshness of the intent. For example, I may be on a lookout to buy a travel ticket for 2 hours, maybe on a lookout to buy a refrigerator for 1 month and maybe on a lookout to buy a house for 2 years. This is a very important behavioral parameter to consider.

   b. **Frequency**: There are many facets of frequency. In a typical RFM segment, frequency is used for defining the loyalty quotient of the user base. For example, the user may visit a news site 3 times per week. This could make him/her a loyal user.

c. **Monetary**: This is usually a historic value of transactions that the user has done. This helps in understanding the behavior vis-à-vis, a price tag and general product and brand affinity.

3. **Rule-based segments**: They are probabilistic in nature and try to categorize a user on behavioral aspects. I will try to showcase a few examples on this:

   a. Example 1: Segment name: Female – a visitor visiting a female fashion site may suggest that the user is a female.

   b. Example 2: Segment name: Intended traveler – a visitor visiting travel and/or hotel website may be construed as a user who may be travelling shortly.

   c. Example 3: Segment name: Potential home buyer – a visitor visiting the real estate project site.

   d. Example 4: Segment name: People who live in Mumbai – this is a user set that lives in Mumbai. This can also be referred to as **geofencing**.

4. **Deterministic segments**: These are usually based on self-declared data by the user.

   a. Example: Segment name: Age 18–22 – This data may be captured when the user is filling a form.

   b. Example: Segment name: Gender male – Could be taken out from CRM that had in turn got the information when the user signed up.

5. **A segment of segments**: This category of segments is defined by set operations (unions, intersections, not and minus). This is usually the case in targeting.

   a. **Unions**: It is the summation of two or more segments, for example, users belonging to the category of intended travelers or females. This segment could be a potential decision-maker.

   b. **Intersection**: They are the common users between two or more segments, for example, the users belonging to intended travelers and females.

   c. **Not**: This is a set operation but usually places a segment in the target level outliers/blacklist for all the good reasons. For example, if a user bought a product, then you do not want to show ads of the same product anymore.

   d. **Minus**: This is typically used when a set of users' needs to be taken out of a segment. For example, potential home buyers – Home buyers will keep the list of potential home buyers intact.

Working with probabilistic segments is usually hampered with overfitting and underfitting scenarios. This has to be calibrated using continuous learning of the segment performance or any other monitoring metric. It is quick to gain accuracy debts and needs to be cleaned from time to time. To manage this problem, many DMPs will erase all data that is older than one month. This, however, creates another set of problems where the campaign needs data from a bigger window. While in-housing the problem, where the data can have a larger life, the problem is magnified by a lot more times, and hence, the segment definitions have to be carefully designed and monitored.

For example, segment on basis of user behavior can be mapped with many definitions. *Figure 3.13* shows how a user behavior that may shift the user from one segment to another during the entire life cycle.

User Life Cycle

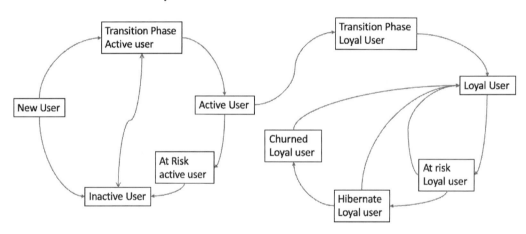

Figure 3.13: *User life cycle data control flow*

Attribution

Attribution is the means to identify the channel of performance that helps in the attainment of a KPI. For a better understanding of this context, one must understand that a marketer deploys various digital channels for business KPI attainment.

For example, in a campaign where the click is the goal and a user clicks on a banner ad. This can also be seen in *Figure 3.14*, where at this point, there are two lines of thought in play:

1. There is a direct line of KPI attainment of click often **called post-click attribution**.

2. The said user may have seen the ad many times earlier that could have modified his/her behavior and persuaded him/her to click the ad this time. This is called **post-view attribution**.

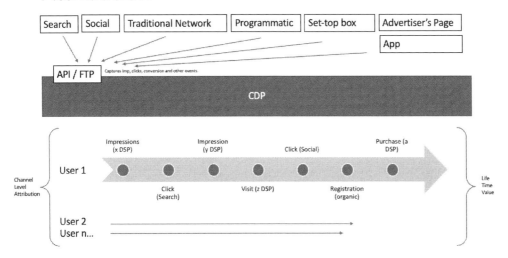

Figure 3.14: Attribution metric

As shown in *Figure 3.14*, the attribution and LTV-based segment (which is usually the subset of RFM-based segments, which have been explained earlier) work with the same dataset. It makes a lot more sense to derive both slices of truth from the same data universe.

From an in-housed CDP perspective, attribution could and should be a part of the CDP scope. This not only reduces the tech stack redundancies but also improves the performance of the overall data.

Note: In all cases, the performance payout is done on basis of attribution data, and hence, this makes it an important aspect of ad-tech.

Overlaying data of different data sources

There are two ways to look at use cases of overlaying of different data sources (of different data owners). DMP/CDPs usually cover this part as an APR report, namely, audience profile report. We also need to consider that a DMP/CDP will usually not give an APR report of the user, but at segment level. The recollection of the definition of first- and third-party data for this to sink in easily is really important.

The first view: For every segment, the third-party data can have users from multiple segments. For example, a segment shopper may constitute 40% male users from data owner Telco, 45% male users from data owner CIBIL (an India government agency that keeps taxpayer's data), and 50% male users from data owner ISP. This is depicted in *Figure 3.15*. Most of the DMPs do not mention data owners beside every segment and represent third-party data against public hierarchies only:

Segment: | Shopper | ▼ |

Third Party Data

Segment Name	%	Data Owner
Male	40%	Telco a
Male	45%	CIBIL
Male	50%	ISP

Figure 3.15: Segment overlap depicting third-party data scenario

In a nutshell, the shopper user set could be approximately 45% male.

The second view: For every segment in the first-party data, the CDP/DMP can host many more users. This usually helps in targeting a large set of users. A sample of such data can be seen in *Figure 3.16*:

Audience

Segment Name	First Party User Count	Third Party User Count	Data Owner
Shopper	30	4000	Telco A
Male	50	10000	CIBIL

Figure 3.16: Segment overlap depicting third-party data scenario

This means that the DMP/CDP has 4,000 users of the shopper segment.

Another use case of data overlay is audience extension. In this example shown in *Figure 3.17*, the third-party attributes of CRM are shared with DMP/CDP within the same http session:

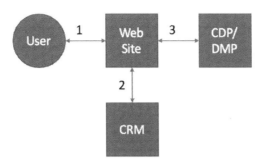

Audience Extension

Figure 3.17: High-level view for audience extension

The steps are as follows:

1. The user opens a website.

2. The website says, login or do social login. Using the authentication pull, the CRM-based attributes load the data onto a form.

3. The attributes are then sent to the CDP/DMP in the same user http session.

4. This is perhaps the best way to share the data along with user consent. This process can also be used to share data between multiple DMP/CDPs.

Recommended Big Data-based architecture for an in-housed CDP

A CDP can be very complex as well as a tricky system to design. Some of the considerations to be taken while designing an in-housed CDP are as follows:

1. Requires a data scheme that can deal with user behavioral data or unstructured data.

2. The ETLs will primarily be responsible for reports and AI/ML-based data manipulations.

3. It will need an AI/ML library to deal with massive unstructured data via parallelism.

4. It needs to be able to trace real-time, near-real-time, and static data as input.

5. All real-time operations have to be complete within 200 ms.

6. The cold start issues may force certain data build-ups initially.

7. We also need to keep in mind the design in order to accommodate easy upgrades on a per platform integration, data source, and client (internal and external) basis.

In an n-tier system delivery modular architecture, a two-tier system can deliver enhanced performance. From a CDP (for that matter, all ad-tech system) where both are required, we always try to design all configuration setups via n-tier systems and all backend apps to work in a two-tier architecture. These two are synced periodically or on an event basis.

Figure 3.18 depicts a high-level architecture for the same:

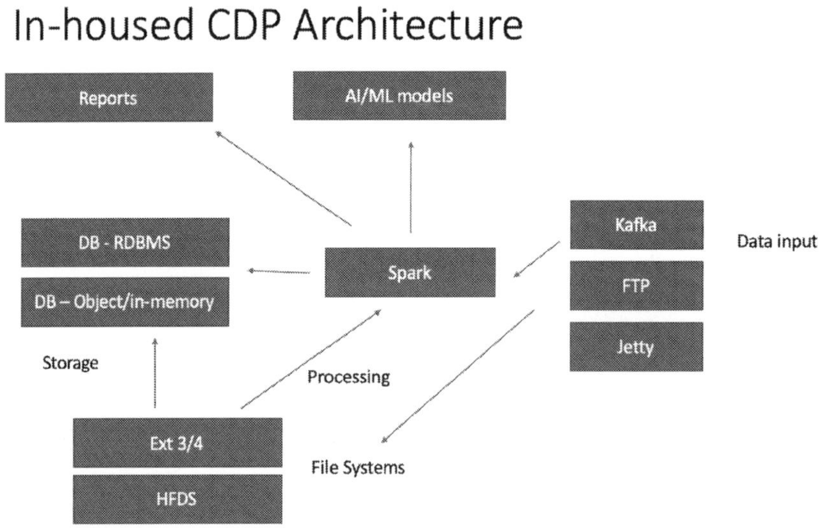

In-housed CDP Architecture

Figure 3.18: *Sample CDP Stack*

One may notice that in certain places, I have mentioned the concept module, and at certain places, I have mentioned the actual package/app that is to be used. One can choose to adopt a set of tech in the vast variety of tech stacks available. I have always noticed that at the end of technology selection, one is usually left with few limited choices. I have mentioned Kafka, Jetty, and Spark because of the multiple numbers of projects my team has executed; most of the times we have ended up choosing them. However, feel free to explore other stacks as well.

The preceding *Figure 3.18* showcases the architecture with the following set of functions, which are as follows:

1. **Kafka, Jetty, and FTP**: These are the several ways in order to get the data into the system via messaging stream, http-based API, and the CSV/XLS file. I have not recommended using a general webserver to capture data due to performance and resource footprint issues. This is also used to drop cookies/pixels, sync data, and carry out required re-directs.

2. **HDFS and Ext3/4**: These are the filesystems that can be used. I have not mentioned YARN or any other resource manager for distributed filesystems to keep a high-level view. However, one needs to look into that aspect as well. One thing that is to be considered is that memory basis IO versus disk-based IO usually have different performance benchmarks. This has to be calibrated with care in different load scenarios.

3. **Spark**: A framework that provides ETL and AI/ML libraries that supports parallelism.

4. **Reports**: Many reports such as APR and so on.

5. **The AI/ML model interface**: It is used by exchange and bidder and other systems from the buy and sell side that will be covered in the upcoming chapters.

I have not mentioned a webserver for UI that is used for configurations and so on, but nevertheless, it also needs to be taken care of.

Challenges of activating data

Nowadays, a good DMP is usually able to effectively activate data to the tune of 50%. There are many factors that make this very challenging, which results in such poor performance. Some of them are as follows:

1. **Bounce rate**: If we try to do extra-long sync hops to sync multiple cookies, it takes over 10 seconds as a whole. Then, in that case, any number of bounce rate will usually break a large rate of sync.

2. **Incognito mode**: In this, the system keeps dropping cookies and keeps syncing them. The problem is that the cookie lasts only during the session.

3. **Third-party cookie block**: This again breaks the third-party cookie sync process at the browser level itself.

4. **User deletion**: The user deletes the cookies at the browse level and others.

Fundamentally, we need 100% synced IDs for the activation to work 100%. As there are many technical and user behavioral factors for the sync to break the activation, it becomes much more challenging.

Conclusion

There are distinct differences between CDP and DMP. But essentially, a CDP is targeted for buy- or sell-side use cases, whereas a DMP is a targeter for data trading and activations. An audience-first approach starts by determining a CDP/DMP blueprint that can help to achieve effective buy or sell functions.

In-housing a CDP is a very important step that should be taken into consideration with utmost care. Not only are the underlying infrastructures complex, but also the supporting modules and external integrations can make it challenging.

The next two chapters explain the supply- and demand-side systems. While some of the text may be independent, an understanding of CDP and data strategies will help build a better understanding of programmatic overall.

Questions

1. Create a checklist of a CDP for demand-side deployment.

2. Create a checklist of a CDP for supply-side deployment.

3. How does a CDP help optimize buys and sells?

Solution

1. The checklist of the CDP for demand-side deployment is as follows:

    *   Ascertain the data universe. Typically, this is the RTB stream. The first-party data also become critical to the CDP design.

    *   Design a mechanism for loop back data, that is, impression, clicks, and so on.

    *   Fix on the AI modules that will be used by the demand-side platform for CPM, CPC, and other funnel metrics.

    *   Ascertain the data activation paradigm.

    *   Fix on the simulation processes.

    The list should help in ascertaining a way to do adopt a CDP for a demand-side platform.

2. The checklist of CDP adoption for sell-side deployment is as follows:

    *   Ascertain the data universe. This is typically auction data.

    *   Design a mechanism for loop back data, that is, impressions, view ability, and so on.

    *   Fix on AI modules for data enrichment, dynamic floor pricing, and/or another target use case.

    *   Fix on a simulation process.

3. A CDP becomes critical for buy and sell at multiple levels. All targeting and audience and media-based AI would come from the CDP. For every auction-based ecosystem, the buyer and seller need to be intelligent. A CDP helps in this intelligence acquisition.

CHAPTER 4

Exchanges, Ad-Servers, and Header Bidding

Introduction

Exchange, ad-servers, and header bidding systems are generally called **Supply-Side Platforms (SSP)**. These terms are also used loosely and are often interchangeable. All these platforms play a specific part in generating advertising revenue for a publisher.

In today's time, publishers face tough situations on the digital front. Traditionally, publishers have made revenue to support content acquisition/production, innovation, and growth. On the digital front, the complex digital marketplace has eaten away a large pie of revenues, and they are losing control of the situation rapidly. This has led to declining revenues and eCPM. For example, Google newsroom, FB newsroom, and so on have started eating into the organic traffic for a news publisher. One may think that a digital-first publisher would be in a better situation, but they constantly find themselves in a riskier zone year after year that comes by. Wherein publishers have started moving onto subscription models, and in turn, these have started to pay off; the fact still remains that less than 10% of the total user base subscribes to paid content services.

One of the primary goals of this book is to help publishers understand the underlying technology and command behind better eCPM in the marketplace. This is done by managing media and audience by tagging them and asking for the best price.

The idea is to explain various supply chains working and the ways and means of optimizing them.

I have tried to keep the text suitable for people who are new to the programmatic world and for the advanced users who may have tried a few things on the audience and want to do the next best thing.

Structure

- Introduction to programmatic:
    - Working of the **Real-Time Bidding (RTB)** protocol
    - Key data in a bid request
- Working of an exchange:
    - Architecture
    - First price- and second-price auction mechanism
    - Mediation – mapping multiple demand sources
    - Supply paths
- Working of an ad-server
    - Working of a header bidding system
    - Client versus server side
- Why competing with DFP became utterly necessary?
- Ad frauds generated by publisher and fraud publisher
- Measurement KPIs and techniques
- Optimization techniques
- Strategic thinking

Objective

A lot of this chapter can be understood without prior knowledge of a CDP. At the same time, I will recommend understanding the concepts of CDP before diving into the depth that is required to make a difference in yield. This will especially be necessary for the latter part of the chapter. For the strategic thinking part of the chapter where the publisher has to play to its strengths to make better revenue, I would recommend doing a speed reading of the next chapter "Bidders and Meta DSPs" to understand the other end of the stick.

I also do not want to touch any platform per se, but the header bidding system topic demands us to cover the topic of DFP. I will recommend getting some understanding of the DFP working to get a better understanding of the header bidding sections.

Finally, as I am a proponent of the audience-first approach, I will try to explain how an audience-first approach can be achieved and how in-housing can benefit a publisher for maximum and sustainable yield.

Introduction to programmatic

Programmatic was designed to automate media sells and media buys. I always find myself trying to oversimplify this topic, but as a matter of fact, it does not do any good for anyone. Anyways, for the ones who do not have first-hand experience in this field, let me try to build the publisher scenario in a few steps:

For example, there is one advertiser and one publisher, as depicted in the following figure:

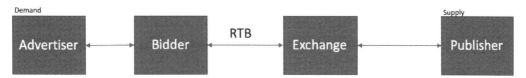

Figure 4.1: *Supply chain*

Following things happen here:

1. RTB is a real-time bidding protocol. In the programmatic world, all the exchange to bidder communication happens via this protocol. It is like two systems talking in their own language. I am giving some context for the continuity sake – but will cover this later in a bit more detail.

    a. **Exchange**: Generated a bid request for the various bidders attached to it and further conducts auctions between various bids received.

    b. **Bidder**: Places bid depending on the demand available. In other words, if a campaign qualifies and a sufficient budget is present, then the bid is placed.

    c. **Bid**: Bidding is done to trade media in real time.

2. So, when a user comes to the publisher's site, usually, the page-load event happens, and subsequently, it fires ad-request toward the demand side. It is called an ad-request when it travels from publisher to exchange and gets converted to a bid request (following RTB protocol) from exchange to demand.

3. The demand side checks for a relevant campaign for the request, and if available, then attempts to buy the media by placing a bid. This process is called bid response.

4. When the bid response comes back to the exchange, the exchange conducts an auction. In this case, because there is only one buyer, any campaign that has bid cost over and above the floor price will win the auction.

5. Whoever wins the auction effectively buys the space for that ad-request, and hence, his/her ad gets placed.

This is the flow for the bid request/repose. With this, the publisher can do the following:

1. The publisher is able to set the floor price.

2. The publisher is able to conduct the auction post receiving the bids.

We still need to be able to configure the ad-space/ad-unit and ad-rendering mechanism.

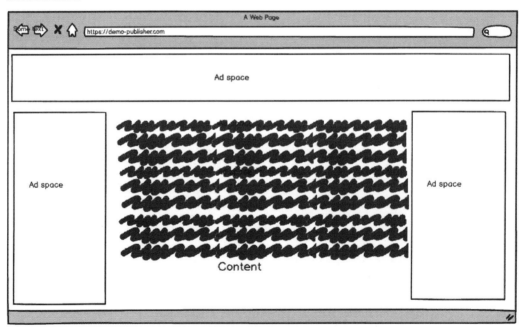

Figure 4.2: *Typical ad-unit placement/positioning of ad-spaces*

Usually, publishers relate to the ad-space from the website perspective. However, from the programmatic perspective, the ad-space is referred to as an ad-unit. The second part is rendering. Usually, the rendering part is done by a publisher-side ad-server. At this point, few more items get attached to *Figure 4.1*, and it now looks as follows:

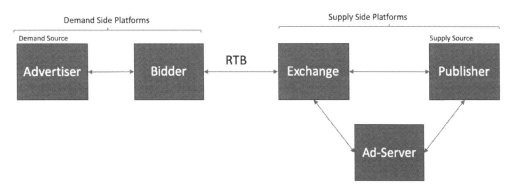

Figure 4.3: *Supply chain*

A publisher typically would configure ad-units in an ad-server along with its rendering code, floor prices, size, content type, and so on.

Note: RTB is only for trading and conducting auctions. The actual ad-rendering is done by the publisher or some publisher-side ad-servers.

So, with this block, a basic ad can get placed with one publisher and advertiser. The next step in scale-up comes when every bidder has multiple advertisers and every exchange has multiple publishers. This is how the SSP acts as an aggregator of publishers.

Note: For the people coming from content management system background, an ad-server is similar to CMS and portal manager plus, in some cases, some audience-level functions. Also, an ad-server works in a true n-tier architecture, which enables it to function in many configurations. To support this kind of modularity, RTB specifications have standard content types that they support.

The following figure depicts a scale-up view of the ecosystem:

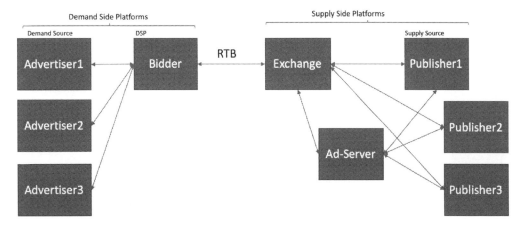

Figure 4.4: *Supply chain*

Programmatic is about trading media using automation to attain scale. The whole ecosystem is designed based on this principle. As it is modular in nature, one can exercise creativity in isolation and then quickly scale, that is, for example, one can make a new interactive content type – such as a video with a follow-on for bot and deploy the feature using the ad-server. However, this also makes the ecosystem patchy if things have not been in check for some time. This high degree of modularity and automation also creates certain challenges for in-housing.

Note: DoubleClick for Publisher (DFP) is one of the popular ad-server and brings many features for monetization for a publisher.

The bidder or DSP also deploys a host of services, but that will be covered in the next chapter. In addition to this, user sync flow happens that works in parallel for user targeting. This stays relevant in the case of Web and mobile Web-based traffic and is not required in the app because it works on persistent IDs. The following figure depicts the foundational working of audience-based ad-serving:

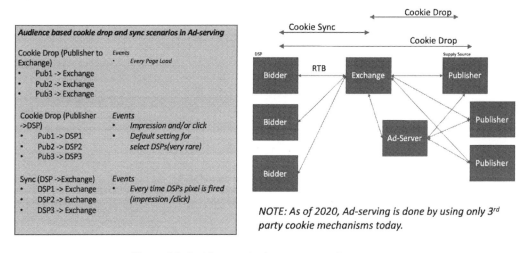

Figure 4.5: Cookie syncs in the programmatic ecosystem

The cookie sync mechanism has been explained in the earlier chapters. As a publisher, the inventory can be sold in an open programmatic ecosystem where all the DSPs are open to bid. The second way is to create a private deal, also referred to as a Private Marketplace (PMP), that will allow a one-on-one deal between the marketer and publisher over RTB.

Working of the Real-Time Bidding (RTB) protocol

RTB is the communication protocol between the exchange and bidder. As ad-servers were used for ad-serving and RTB came in later, the publishers adopted ad-server-based mechanisms to initiate RTB requests. The flow does not use all the features of the protocols many times. This was an easy migration to an auction-based mechanism. However, a programmatic approach enables publishers to maximize yield using the auction. This is important for the publisher to understand for various reasons:

1. A DSP uses RTB stream-based data for media planning. An enriched RTB steam helps the publisher to position its media and audience in the marketer's media. An enriched RTB stream is attained by populating the RTB metadata. A good-quality RTB metadata will help publishers achieve higher eCPM and fill.

2. A DSP/bidder usually deploys two-stage mechanisms to buy the media. The first is budget and target parameters (geo, handset, user segment, blacklist, and so on) based filtering, and the second is the AI/ML layer that helps the DSP to ascertain the right price for the KPI that it needs to cater to. If the publisher can position the media and audience for these two things, then a publisher will be in a better position to maximize yield.

3. RTB stream on the exchange side becomes auction data, which is an aggregate of responses by multiple DSPs/bidders. Auction data can be used to see the marketers who are trying to buy inventory and at what price. This data can further be used for an adequate balance between the floor price and fill.

> **Note: From an economic perspective, this is a mix of price elastic and law of demand and supply. If we can plot the demand, then we can arrive at an adequate price.**

RTB was built for machine-to-machine communication, that is, to understand it better, we need to understand the dimensions that it covers in this communication. The exchange to bidder communication, also known as bid request, contains many data blocks. Some of the key attributes represented by the data blocks (objects) are as follows:

Key data in a bid request

1. **Source**
   a. It tells about the source of the media.
   b. Ensures that transactions can be mapped between all the exchanges and DPSs by providing one ID for the request.

2. **Regs**
   a. It tells about the various regulations that would apply to the request.
   b. There is also an option to add exchange/source to specific information.

3. **Imp**

   a. It tells about the ad-unit.

   b. Tells about the display stack that is being used.

   c. It also tells about the bid floor. This is one of the most important attributes to be set for eCPM optimization represented by the "bidfloor" attribute.

   d. Tells about the user browser.

   e. Has Metric, Banner, Video, Audio, Native, and Pmp as child objects.

4. **Metric**

   a. It talks about the various metrics that the ad-unit carries such as viewability, click-through rate, and so on.

   b. Also tells if the exchange is the original source of media. The same thing can also be achieved by ads.txt.

5. **Banner**

   a. It tells about the format with the format object.

   b. Tells about the position of the ad-unit on the publisher's site.

   c. Tells about the blacklisted category of the creatives.

   d. It talks about the linkage to the video.

6. **Video**

   a. It talks about the video protocols that the creative could support.

   b. Tells about the height x width x mime specification of the video.

   c. Tells about the minimum duration and maximum duration of the content.

   d. Tells about the blocked categories.

   e. It has a lot of parameters on the playback, companion content, and so on.

7. **Audio**

   a. Tells about the minimum duration, maximum duration, and mimes.

   b. Also tells about bit rate and so on.

8. **Native**

   a. It usually combines multiple creative objects with a specific or custom rendering format. This is usually taken as a payload with native ad specs.

   b. Tells about the blocked creative attributes.

9. **Format**

   a. Tells about the formats using an array signifying that an ad-unit can support multiple sizes in banners.

   b. This makes banners a relatively easy content type to fill in.

10. **PMP (Private Market Place)**

    a. Tells about the direct deals in a private and public format.

    b. Has a Deal object as the child object.

11. **Deal**

    a. Tells the floor price of the deal.

    b. Tells about the list of advertiser domains that are allowed to bid for the media.

    c. Tells about the deal ID.

12. **Site**

    a. Tells the publisher name and domain.

    b. Tells the category, section category, and page category.

    c. Tells about the URL of the page where the ad will be shown along with the referral URL.

    d. Tells about the search string.

    e. Tells about the privacy policy.

    f. Tells about the keywords.

    g. Has Content and Keyword as child objects.

    h. Tells if the site is optimized for mobile.

13. **App**

    a. Tells about the app-based inventory.

b. Tells if the app is free or paid.

c. Tells about the content, publisher, page category, section category, and category.

d. Tells about the bundle, domain, and store UTL.

e. Tells about the app name.

14. Publisher

a. Tells about the publisher.

b. Tells about the category.

c. Tells about the publisher domain.

15. Content

a. Tells about the content where the ad is going to be shown.

b. It can be in the form of audio, video, and so on.

c. Tells about the episode, album, ISRC, context, content rating, media rating, keywords, and so on.

16. Producer

a. Tells about the producer. In case the content is syndicated and has multiple publishers, this info comes in handy.

b. Tells about the category and domain of the producer.

17. Device

a. Tells about the IP, make, model, OS, height x Width, screen size, language, and so on.

b. Tells about the geofence API that it would support.

c. Tells about device ID, mac address, platform device ID, and advertiser ID.

d. Tells about connections, carriers, and so on.

e. Has a Geo object as a child.

18. Geo

a. Tells about the latitude, longitude, last position, region, country, city, zip, and so on.

b. Tells about the accuracy estimates as well.

19. User

a. Tells about the exchange-specific user ID.

b. Tells about the buyer ID, gender, year of birth, and so on.

c. There is also an option to send custom data that was set by the bidder in the user cookie.

d. Has Data and Geo objects as a child.

20. Data

a. Tells about the exchange given name of the data provider.

b. Has a Segment object as a child.

21. Segment

a. Tells all the segments about where the user belongs.

The bid request, if it clears the bidder targeting options and the floor price threshold, is responded to by the `BidResponse` object. The key points of the bid response are as follows:

1. BidResponse

a. Tells about the bid ID that corresponds to the bid request.

b. Has SeatBid as a child object.

2. SeatBid

a. Tells about the advertiser ID who is bidding.

b. Tells if the impression can be won in a group or individually.

c. Has Bid as a child object.

3. Bid

a. Tells about impression ID that corresponds to the bid request.

b. Tells about the price that the advertiser is willing to pay.

c. Tells about the nurl, burl, and lurl for impression/win, billing, and loss tracking purposes.

d. Tells about the adm, which contain markup-based notices.

e.   Tells about the preloaded ads, advertiser domains, bundles, campaign ID, creative ID, tactic ID, category, attributes describing creatives, and so on.

f.   Tells about the creative specs.

g.   Tells about the wait time for the bidder's willingness to get back the win notification.

h.   Tells about the deal ID.

The combination of the bid request and bid response becomes auction data. This is a very important data source and forms the data universe for the CDP. This is used for eCPM and revenue optimization.

Note: RTB was designed to trade data and media, but due to data corporatization by giants, the RTB is reduced to media trade only. Further to that, even the media trade happens with minimal data, which is limited by the ad-request. Please check earlier chapters to see the use cases of auction data.

Working of an exchange

Exchange is the edge of the SSP stack that the publisher would deploy. Please refer to *Figure 4.6* that shows a publisher can be attached to multiple exchanges, and the exchanges could be attached to multiple DSPs:

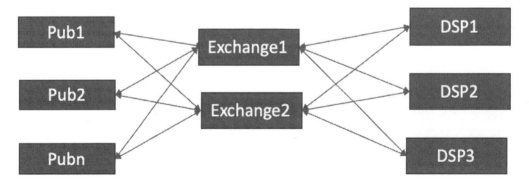

Figure 4.6: High-level exchange view

An exchange does two primary activities, which are as follows:

1.   It tries to source the demand from as many DSPs as possible. In some cases, to optimize the infra cost, an exchange may want to send out bid requests to select DSPs. In advance cases of optimization, an exchange could send different content categories of a bid request to different DSPs based on the historic demand fulfillment.

2. Once the exchange has received the bid requests from all the DSPs, it conducts the auction and forwards the win to the publisher site for rendering.

In a pure programmatic world, an exchange is a straightforward module that will fetch demand. However an exchange is usually configured behind an ad-server because a lot of demand sources can also work with both tag-based demand and RTB. This also creates a requirement of mediation control between multiple demand tag systems.

A quick comparison between a tag- and RTB-based system from the publisher's perspective is given as follows:

Case	Tag	RTB
Dynamic floor price	Cannot provide.	Can be provided.
Enriched metadata	NA.	Can be provided.
Ease of integration	4 of 5.	2 of 5.
Audience-led media sell	Limited.	Extensive feature set.
Target demand sources	Has to be done in the waterfall model.	Can be done in parallel.
Latency	800 ms – this limits the waterfall from 3–5 tag-based demand partners.	800 ms – can call for any number of demand partners.
Revenue potential	Due to the waterfall model, revenue realization is not optimized.	Due to the parallel call to demand partners and subsequent auction mechanism, revenue potential is optimal.

Table 4.1: Tag versus RTB working for an ad-request

In today's scenario, typically, an SSP(Exchange plus Ad-Server) will support RTB and tag-based demand sources. Advance exchange may go further and give out features for audience-based demand sourcing.

Note: Tag-based integration is where the advertiser or the demand source places a JS tag onto the publisher site to directly render the ad. However, if the tag does not get the fill, then it gives a pass-back to the ad-server. This flow gets repeated to accommodate multiple tag-based demand sources.

Architecture

Every exchange tries to provide some uniqueness in its offering, and there are over 100 exchanges today that may differ in some way or the other. However, I will try to depict an ideal scenario that would cover all publishers' interests. The primary interests of the publisher are as follows:

1. The exchange, in the data privacy paradigm, becomes a processor and needs the exchange to be able to manage user consent.

    a. As the exchange passes the data to the bidder and various ad-network, it needs to also behave as a gateway to the user consent.

    b. Exchange needs to ensure that if the user has not given consent, then it should ensure that the DSP -> exchange sync is broken, and the user object is ripped of any ID that the publisher is passing.

2. The exchange has to enrich the metadata, so the DSP has a fair idea of what it is buying, and also the DSP finds the media and audience interesting in terms of detail availability.

3. The exchange has to optimize the revenue potential of the publisher. The most effective way to do so is by managing the floor price adequately. Primarily, two things need to be done for revenue optimization:

    a. To ensure that the publisher gets the best eCPM, that is, effective cost per mile.

    b. To ensure that the publisher gets the most fill.

4. The exchange needs to manage the user experience by enforcing strict latency-related parameters. Typically, an exchange needs to be able to render the ad in 800 ms.

5. In a world that is dominated by the DFP, the exchange should provide a consolidated view on revenue realization in increments and as a whole.

Like I said before, exchanges have many configurations. This is because of the rapid advancement in the RTB ecosystem in the last 5 years or so. Secondly, the exchanges usually try to accommodate large publishers by doing certain levels of customizations. So, bearing that in mind, I will try to give out an ideal design of an exchange that a publisher should seek.

The following figure describes the various modules and interfaces an exchange would have to serve in the new age RTB ecosystem:

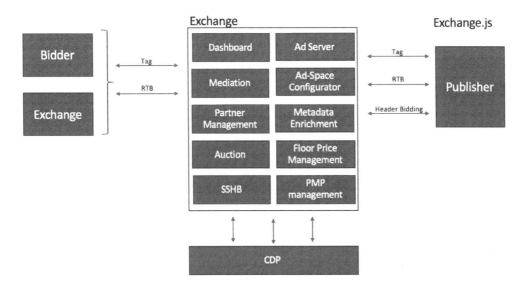

Figure 4.7: *High level view of Exchange(SSP)*

The description of the various modules and interfaces are as follows:

1. **Exchange.js** does three things on the publisher side:

    a. It drops cookies in case of Web and mobile Web, and it captures advertiser ID or device ID for the ad serving a purpose. This is described in *Figure 4.5*. The first and second steps, from the publisher's side to audience-based ad-serving, are to identify the user and generate the ad-request with the user ID also known as cookie ID or device ID.

    b. It renders the ad on the publisher site. This is an extension of the ad-server that is part of the exchange. In a legacy system, this can also be a standalone system. Ad-serving would typically support certain content types such as image, video, audio. In the case of native, it will support a combination of video, image, and text. In the case of VAST, it would support video playback with features of event capture such as 5-second play, 30-second play, full video view, and so on. The ad-server could also become more creative to enable formats for a brand survey, content seeding, and so on.

    c. Generation of ad-request is the first step to call out for demand. In the case of client-side header bidding systems, a client-based module will also conduct secondary auctions.

A new-age exchange should deliver a new-age set of features. In-housing demands an integrated feature set for managing inventory. The various modules for inventory monetization are as follows:

1. Dashboards are divided into three parts – usage, revenue, and insights. Some of the reports that exchange can throw out are as follows:

    a. **Usage**: These impact the direct cost to host exchange, hence becomes important. This is also directly proportional to the revenue; hence, a balance of cost versus revenue has to be achieved. Some of the usage dashboards could be as follows:

        i. The ad-request is generated on per page, per content, or per group site basis. Also, this could be bifurcated between geo, device, and daypart. Such data can be used to bifurcate various yields on a usage basis.

        ii. The traffic that was generated to source demand on a per DSP and exchange basis. This can be further utilized to throttle traffic depending on the demand source to save cost.

        iii. eCPM versus fill is an important metric giving a sense of the long tail that could have gotten generated but not bringing goodness to anyone. This data can be used to manage longtail by adding or removing ad-spaces.

    b. **Revenue**: It is a function of yield (represented by effecting cost per mile known as eCPM) and fills.

        i. Revenue optimization can be done by identifying media and audience segments and ascertaining adequate prices for them. Such blocks that can fetch higher eCPM will eventually increase the overall revenue.

        ii. Revenue potential versus user experience is an important metric to monitor. A revenue line based on poor user experience will not be sustainable.

    c. **Insights**: It depends on the management goals. I have seen executives overdoing the insight piece, but if this is aligned to short- and long-term goals, then such data is always of interest.

        i. RFM-based loyal user base can be used to understand the content consumption patterns. These patterns can be further used for content planning and advertiser-based content seeding.

      ii.   Correlating the yield patterns to external events helps to use external factors to increase yield with minimal effort.

     iii.   Tracking the top marketer's demand can help improve yield.

     iv.   Tracking the content uptake can help understand the shift in user behavior in content consumption.

2. **Ad-Server**: It is used for supporting various content types for the publisher. Some of the content types are as follows:

   a.   Banner

      i.   XHTML text ads

      ii.   HTML banner ad

     iii.   JS ad (a valid XHTML)

     iv.   iframe

   b.   Beyond banners, there are a whole lot of things that an ad-server can manage. Please check the RTB specification for the following:

      i.   **Creative attributes**: For example, user interactive/embedded games and so on.

      ii.   **Expandable directions**: For example, left, right, and so on.

     iii.   **API frameworks**: For example, VPAID 1.0, MRAID-3, and so on.

      iv.   **Video linearity**: For example, linear/in-stream and so on.

      v.   **Protocols**: For examples, VAST 1.0 wrapper and so on.

      vi.   **Playback method**: Initiates on page load with sound on, and so on.

     vii.   **Content delivery methods**: Streaming, progressive, and so on.

    viii.   **Content context**: For example, video, games, music, and so on.

      ix.   And so on.

3. **Mediation**: It handles the bidding control flow.

   a.   Mediation is the control flow to source the demand for the publisher. Some examples of the mediation could be as follows:

    i. RTB -> tag1 -> tag2 -> in-house

    ii. Tag1 -> RTB -> in-house

    iii. Direct

    iv. Tag1 -> tag2 -> in-house and so on.

    v. There are three types of demand sources that exchange can cater to. Every demand source has a way to interact with other sources.

    vi. **RTB based:** All RTB channels work in parallel. The RTB demand is catered on a per request/response basis. This means that the exchange can choose to reject any and every response. This also includes the PMP.

    vii. **Tag-based:** If a tag-based request can fetch the demand, then the ad is served, and in case the tag request does not get the demand, the control is passed back to the mediation.

    viii. **Direct/in-house:** This is usually the last phase of the mediation flow. This corresponds to a direct deal that will be served by the ad-server or the in-house campaign that is there to cater to the un-filled ad-request.

4. **Ad-space configurator**: Ad-space relates to the type of mime specifications the site administrator is willing to show along with its floor price.

    a. Some of the formats and their behavior are as follows:

        i. Example: Multiple sizes of images.

        ii. Example: VAST or video.

        iii. Example: Native.

        iv. As the RTB can support requests in multiple formats and various formats fetch different eCPM, the operator may wish to optimize given the demand.

    b. Ad-space also includes floor price.

    c. Such configurations are used to generate bid requests toward DSPs/bidders.

    d. The exchange may even want to group the ad-space to opt for easy management.

5. **Partner management**: Exchange connects with various demand sources and publishers. Publisher to demand source is usually in many-to-many formats.

This calls for judicial care for invoicing and data privacy.

6. **Metadata enrichment**: There are over 220 data fields in the RTB request. Due to competing attributes, all of them cannot be filled. As a publisher, one must understand that enrichment of metadata is directly proportional to eCPM and fills. This can be attained by using AI engines to pull the content and populate the RTB attributes.

7. **Server-Side Header Bidding (SSHB)**: SSHB ensures that multiple demand sources can be catered to in a single client request. This is done to complete the DFP.

8. **Private Marketplace (PMP)**: At times, publishers and marketers strike a deal for direct buy. Such an arrangement is enabled by the PMP feature. In this, the exchange generates a deal ID, and the buyer then needs to source the supply from this deal ID.

Note: prebid.org is a header bidding project that caters to open-source connectors for various demand sources. Technically, SSHB is much better than that of client-side header bidding. This is because of the latency that is produced by the client-side header bidding system. Also, in case of SSHB, the scope to source the demand increases.

PMP: The PMP construct imitates the traditional block buy of the older times. They were very popular, but because the supply is also available in the open market and usually at a lower prices, PMPs are losing on popularity.

First- and second-price auction mechanism

Auction mechanics are straightforward; that is, it is the implications that can get tricky at times. Exchanges in the programmatic ecosystem started with second-price auctions. Around the mid of 2019, exchanges started to shift to the first-price auction.

For example:

For a bid request r.

Advertiser a -> bid 1 USD

Advertiser b -> bid 1.1 USD

Advertiser c-> bid 1.2 USD

In the case of the second-price auction:

Winner -> Advertiser c and pays 1.1

In the second-price auction, the highest bid wins but ends up paying the second-highest price. In case there is only one advertiser for the bid, depending on the exchange, the second highest could be the floor prices or the bid itself.

In case of the first-price auction:

Winner -> Advertiser c and pays 1.2

In the first-price auction, the highest bidder pays what he has bid.

First-price auction mechanics are publisher-friendly, and the second-price auctions are advertiser-friendly.

In the ecosystem that works on media commissions, the media prices are usually layered with commissions. A second-price auction makes it almost impossible to figure out the commission margin in the actual bid. This problem, to some extent, gets solved in the first-price auction mechanisms.

> **Note: In theory, the first-price auction should fetch better revenue for the publisher. However, most of the DSPs today deploy the bid shading algorithm, which is an AI-powered logic that constantly tries to bring down the media and audience price to the floor price level.**

Mediation – mapping multiple demand sources

A publisher looks at the exchange as a demand source. On the other hand, an advertiser looks at the exchange as a supply source. The exchange itself is a facade of supply-to-demand connections. The mediation module typically maps the control of this flow to the source of demand. Some general rules of mediation system are as follows:

1. Every step should be able to source demand.

2. Every step of the mediation can complete within itself but cannot compete between different steps.

3. If a step cannot source demand, then the control moves to the next step.

4. As a publisher yield manager, I would want to keep the higher floor price-based sources on top and go down in descending order.

5. In general, the control will not move to post the in-house campaign. This means that even if mediation flow is configured to have other demand sources beyond in-house campaigns, those demand sources will be unreachable.

Some mediation flow examples are shown in the following figure:

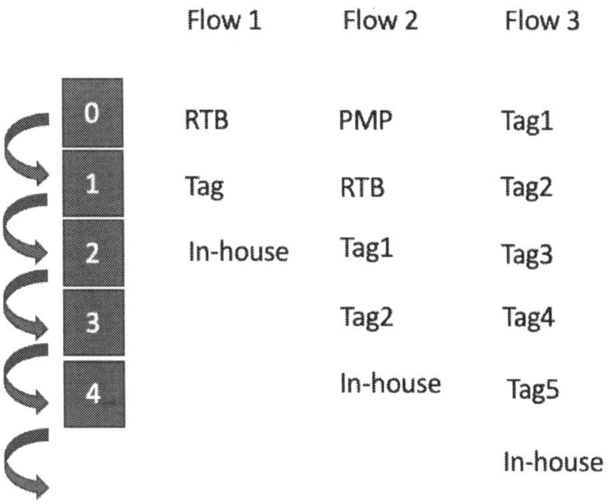

	Flow 1	Flow 2	Flow 3
0	RTB	PMP	Tag1
1	Tag	RTB	Tag2
2	In-house	Tag1	Tag3
3		Tag2	Tag4
4		In-house	Tag5
			In-house

Figure 4.8: Mediation flow

For the most optimized revenue in the open market, one has to configure the mediation for RTB and in-house only. The tag-based demand sources usually do not fetch optimal eCPM because it is impossible to give the right order of execution. A publisher still works with tags due to ease of integration.

Note: All publishers should get out of tag-based demand source scenarios. It results in minimal amount of goodness. They need to opt for RTB-based demand sources for best revenue.

Supply paths

The programmatic ecosystem can support very complex supply paths. It is important to understand how this happens before getting into what is happening. There are three perspectives:

1. The programmatic ecosystem is mostly paid by advertisers, and hence, a DSP, to make more money, also owns an exchange by doing a reverse integration. This has resulted in a lot of integrated DSP and exchange stack.

2. So, when an integrated exchange and DSP runs out of demand, the exchange part can look at another exchange or DSP for demand. This enables a possibility request hops within the RTB demand sources of supply path that is only limited by the 800 ms timeout.

3. A publisher looks at reaching maximum advertisers by injecting bid requests in multiple exchanges. This makes a publisher's inventory available to the marketer via multiple paths and trade desk/DSPs.

DFP is one of the most popular and one of the oldest ad-servers in our programmatic ecosystem. Google's stack of DFP -> Adx -> DBM covers ad-server, exchange, and DSP. This makes Google an owner of the end-to-end supply path from publisher to advertiser. In a non-ideal world, where Google or any player who owns the complete supply path at scale could end up giving first look advance to its own supply path based on-demand sources. This kind of an end-to-end supply path would create two scenarios:

1. This supply path could prefer sourcing demand from its own DSP over other DSPs. This would finally result in revenue loss for the publisher and ROI loss for the advertiser.

2. An end-to-end supply path can push both marketers and publishers to create an unreasonable margin for themselves.

In recent times, some of the best auditors while auditing the programmatic supply chains could not identify all the paths. This means that there is a revenue leak by design, and one must be mindful of such scenarios. Some of the supply paths can be seen in the following figure:

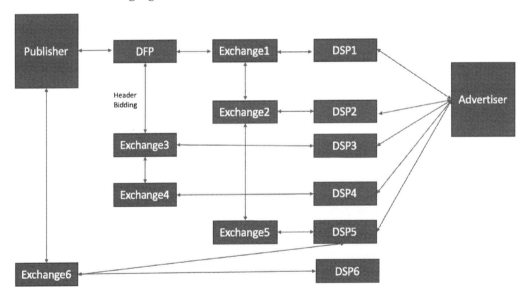

Figure 4.9: Supply chain

Advertisers usually use **Supply Path Optimization (SPO)** algorithm in the DSP to identify the best path to adopt for the said inventory. Hence, it is in the best interest of the publisher to map all the various supply paths. This is necessary to control the end-user price.

Note: As of June 2020, it is estimated that for every 100 USD that an advertiser spends, around 50 USD reaches the publishers. This is in contrast to 85 USD that a publisher gets in print-based advertising. This has generated a sense of frustration for both marketers and publishers. Many industry veterans believe that the interim player's revenue model is simply not sustainable. I think that this ecosystem needs an overhaul in the way these supply paths are managed.

Working of an ad-server

An ad-server primarily participates in the SSP stack to handle the content housing and its rendering functionalities. As the content rendering and content housing can be done in two different systems, the programmatic ecosystem mandates to use of standardized specifications for ad-serving. Standardization of content formats is the only way to attain scale. However, if a publisher wants to test out with a more creative format, then using the ad-server constructs one can achieve that. Gaming players constantly try out new formats. In a generic format, this can be seen as a three-layer system. Usually, a creative is loosely coupled and served by the edge or CDN. This is done to manage the performance of the site. The modular design of the ad-server is depicted in the following figure:

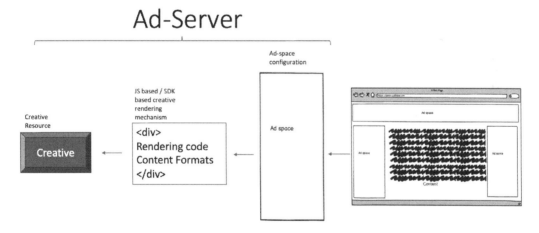

Figure 4.10: Basic working of an ad-server

The components in *Figure 4.10* are as follows:

1. **Ad-space configuration**: This represents the content type, size, mime, format, and so on that the ad-space would show. In certain cases, the ad-space also carries information of the category, blacklist category, keywords, and so on.

2. **Rendering**: It is usually a piece of code (SDK for apps and JS for Web and mobile Web), which will use the ad-space configuration and render the creative in the relevant window. The ad-space configuration can also carry the rendering template making the rendering functionality configurable.

3. **Creative**: This is the content – image, video, audio, and so on – that is finally shown to the users.

Usually, the configuration and rendering functionality is tightly bound by the publisher, and the creative is configured by the advertiser via the campaign. In case of direct demand, a publisher could also host the creatives.

> **Note: This concept works with programmatic TV, OTT, DOOH, and so on. In fact, if one wants to get a media into programmatic, then you just need an ad-server along with auction mechanics that can make inventory tradable.**

There are various measurement metrics of usage. These metrics are around the following:

1. Usage and configuration of creatives.

2. Performance of the creatives.

Working of a header bidding system

It is important to understand the reason for header bidding before getting into the working of it. Publishers have been using DFP from almost the beginning of ad-tech ecosystem existence. With time, DFP, Adx, and DBM/DV360 became monopolistic in nature by dominating the supply chain itself. This made it hard for publishers to introduce any competition to this supply chain. Eventually, publishers realized that by creating more supply chains, they could get better revenues. They were designed to compete with DFPs. One of the popular projects that provide a lot of plug-ins for demand partners using header bidding mechanics is prebid.org. It is a tag-based system that helps source demand from various DSPs.

Figure 4.11 depicts a client-side header bidding scenario.

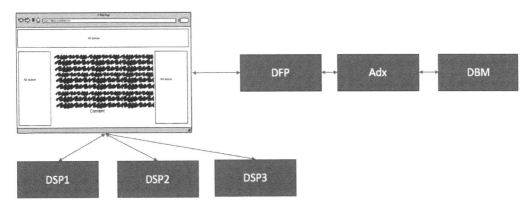

Figure 4.11: *High-level view of client-side header bidding*

There are two modes in which header bidding systems can happen. Client-side and SSHB systems are two ways in which this can work. The working of the client-side header bidding system as depicted in the preceding figure is as follows:

1. When the page loads, the browser fires a request to DSPs. This is usually a tag-based system, and it originates from the browser.

2. When the browser gets the response back, it is forwarded to the DFP.

3. DFP further sources the demand and competes with the bid from the header bidding system.

Note: We can also use the RTB protocol to generate a bid request from the browser itself, but that would become very cumbersome for the browser.

There is only one difference in the SSHB. This is depicted in the following figure:

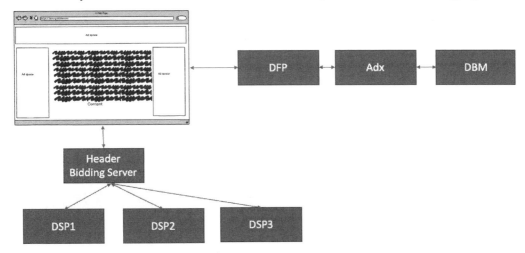

Figure 4.12: *High-level view of the server-side header bidding scenario*

The difference is that the browser, in the case of **SSHB**, gives out one call to the server, and the server can then do multiple waterfalls or parallel calls.

Note: The rule for tag and RTB is still applicable.

This construct can have two levels of auctions. The first-level auction is conducted at the header bidding side with the various demand sources. Once the request is forwarded to the DFP, the primary auction takes place between the header bidding and DFP-based demand.

Client versus server side

Even though there are many similarities in the outcome of the two ways header bidding can be done, the primary differences come in the flexibility and scalability to achieve better yields.

The few cases of flexibility and scalability are as follows:

1. A client, which is the browser or the app, cannot handle the RTB protocol's complexity. Even if it manages to work with a scale-down version on RTB, the mere depth of features would include ad-unit configuration, conducting the secondary auction, ping waits, and so on. This is way too much for the client to handle. For these reasons, clients always choose SDK or tag-based ad-request formats.

2. On the other hand, SSHB can use RTB and tag mechanics to source demand. This makes demand sourcing possible at scale.

3. The client-side header bidding is extremely popular because of the ease it brings. It does not take over a few days to implement such a system.

Note: I usually recommend starting with the client side to get a sense of how HB works and then migrate to SSHB to attain scale. Also, explore SSHB solutions that will source demand of RTB. This will give higher yields.

Why competing with DFP became utterly necessary?

A publisher makes revenue on yield and scale. Both of them are dependent on the kind of supply chain that is available and its performance. A buyer today buys inventory on various KPIs of CMP, CPC, CPA, retargeting, and so on. This means that CPM kind of buyer's KPI would give a scale for the publisher and CPA or retargeting kind of KPIs can give much higher yield for the publisher. Easier said than done, these kinds of optimizations require enormous amounts of data and analysis. This requires log-level data to find the overlapping user and audience segments and further do ad-request-level floor price management.

DFP is a part of a Google-owned and managed supply chain. By design, DFP does not share log-level data. As the supply chain itself is advertiser-driven and middle party-owned, it is in its interest to keep the advertiser's price tag high and publisher's revenue low. This is the only way to make good margins.

With that in mind, when publishers had yields dropping year-on-year, they wanted to challenge the supply chain itself by bringing more demand sources in parallel to the supply chain. Header bidding's client-side version was a construct that was easy and showed some uplift to the revenues.

Google's supply chain then introduced exchange bidding. Google's exchange bidding creates similar parallel demand sources that are provided by the header bidding. This mechanic still keeps both the auctions to happen with the Google supply chain. The mere introduction of such mechanics indicates the intent to keep the pricing control within the Google supply chain.

> **Note: Today, DSPs deploy the SPO to figure out the best path within multiple paths generated by the header bidding systems. So, if a publisher is not using header bidding properly, then he/she may end up losing revenue.**

Ad-frauds generated by publisher and fraud publisher

There are two categories of frauds that happen from the publisher's side. A publisher who goes by the "honesty" code should take steps to deal with both. The two categories are as follows:

1. A fraud that happens due to internal controllable factors such as bots and impression calls.

   a. When a bot comes to the site and triggers the page load event, the subsequent ad-requests get fired.

   b. A publisher could identify the nurl/burl and fire them at will to generate two scenarios.

      i. Create a scenario in which the bidder registers many hits for one actual hit.

      ii. Create a scenario in which multiple advertisers think that their ad is shown where only one advertiser's ad was shown.

2. A fraud happens by the external factors where an entity misuses the identity or control flow.

   a. There are many ways to do this. One such common way is to spoof the domain and register as a publisher with a different billing identity with an exchange. The advertiser thinks that he/she is buying traffic from a reliable publisher, but in actual, the case is different.

   b. The exchange itself is fraud and giving 100% fraud traffic by representing a group of fake publishers.

In both cases, a marketer loses money without any ROI gains. In the first case, the inventory buy is done for a machine. However, the money still goes to the publisher. In the second case, the marketer does not get any ROI, and the money does not even go to the publisher. The bigger problem that makes the situation worse is that the middle party such as exchanges, DSPs, and agencies do not have any incentive to solve this.

However, in all scenarios, a publisher could end up losing credibility. Hence, it is in the publisher's interest to give quality inventory to the marketer at all times.

Measurement KPIs and techniques

There are many things in today's digital ecosystem that a publisher needs to monitor and improve for sustainable revenue. A simpleton argument for a publisher can be – "I only care about revenue." This does more harm than good. Anyways, I always try to break every measurement metric into usage and revenue. This can be broken down as follows:

1. **Usage**

   a. **Loyalty**: Repeat, frequency, and so on.

   b. **Content:** Product profile, trend, and so on.

   c. Bounce rates.

   d. **User experience**: Article read and content viewed, and so on.

   e. Session duration.

2. **Revenue**

   a. **Yield**: Segments (geo, handset, and so on) versus eCPMs.

   b. Demand scoping.

   c. Fill %

One problem that I have seen in the preceding model is that it becomes impossible to justify the cost of attaining user loyalty. This reason can easily derail content planning and recommendation among other core content business aspects.

In another metric, a publisher could look at three aspects to stay in a positive cash flow:

1. How much money does it cost to acquire a user?

2. How much money does it cost to provide service to a user?

3. How much money does a user make?

One just needs to reach where LTV > acquisition + service equation to be cash positive. If done properly, then there is usually a trend/pattern to this.

This is by far the best model to have a sustainable business. Of course, one may need to look at this data at a granular level to understand the range. For example, there will be different user acquisition costs on a segment basis. Similarly, there will be different LTV on a per-user segment basis. The granularity needs to happen to create segment-based insights.

Optimization techniques

Optimization is a balance between what a publisher has to offer versus what a marketer is seeking. There are primarily two things that a publisher can do in a monetization scenario:

1. Can define the inventory by enriching the RTB metadata. The best-case scenario for a marketer is to know as much as possible about the audience and the media. This will help the marketer in the following:

    a. **Brand safety**: A properly categorized RTB media and audience help the marketer to understand the context. This can be used if the media and audience's fitment can be obtained in the RTB request.

    b. **Target filtering**: An enriched request helps the marketer to plan the campaign better.

2. Once the publisher has put the best foot forward to showcase the media and audience, the next thing to do is to put the right price tag.

    a. Floor price indicates the media and audience rating.

    b. Understanding the demand that the request can pull can also affect the rating.

c. External factors such as holidays, events, and so on can affect the rating.

d. A granular level of understanding of the media and audience can help in asking for the right price.

The following figure explains the flow of the optimization mechanics:

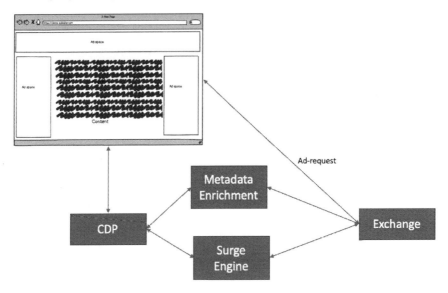

Figure 4.13: CDP-led data enrichment and dynamic floor pricing with RTB stream

The preceding figure works in the following way:

1. The CDP helps to make segments (the granular part) and understand the demand, eCPM, and external factors.

2. **Metadata enrichment**: It is an NLP-based engine that helps in populating the RTB request's metadata.

3. **Surge engine**: It is a component that manages the floor price on a per-request basis. It uses auction data and AI/ML algorithms and determines the optimal price.

Strategic thinking

Some of the key things that have happened in the industry in recent times are as follows:

1. Exchanges shifted from second- to first-price auction. This was supposed to be publisher-friendly, but no revenue increment was attained by any set of meaningful publishers.

2. The marketer does not know the publisher's price in the open RTB ecosystem. On top of that, PMPs have become more expensive than open RTB. Hence, agencies and marketers today are shifting their respective buys from PMP to open RTB.

3. Google constantly tries to keep all auction control within its own supply chain.

By various estimates, the supply chain leaves publishers with 30–50% of the ad-money. This means that for every 1 USD, about 30–50c reaches the publisher. It is an apparent deduction that the supply chain favors the buyer and the interim players. Some analyses on the preceding points are as follows:

1. The shift from the second- to first-price auction mechanics should have boosted revenues from 30 to 100% for publishers. However, DSPs deploy strong bid shading algorithms to constantly put download pressure on pricing. The result is that the buy price gets pushed to the floor levels.

2. PMP construct imitates the block buys. Block buys have always fetched premiums. However, in the new age, the marketer now understands that the media and audience that are available in PMP are also available in open RTB at a lower price. This has made the marketer move from PMP/direct deals to open RTB.

3. The only advantage that Google gets in controlling the auction is that it can give a first-look advantage to its supply chain. This should be viewed carefully on a case-to-case basis to ascertain what kind of dent the construct is making on the overall revenues.

The other two aspects that stare at publishers are about data and users. They are as follows:

1. In today's world of DMPs and Google, a publisher is losing ground on the data front. In a generic ad-request, a publisher does not even define media properly, let alone defining the data. Even if he/she manages to enrich the metadata, a good chance is that the exchange will rip off the data packet before forwarding it to the DSP.

2. The new regulations of user privacy have put publishers in a position where he/she can act as the data custodians. This makes managing data mandatory.

I have also realized that where marketers deploy heavy AI stacks for better buys, publishers, on the other end, are relatively using primitive tools to guard revenues. What I have concluded so far is that publishers have to own the SSP end of the supply chain. They also have to enrich the SSP with data and AI to claim the fair share of ad-money. They also have to deploy AI to fight for better revenue.

Conclusion

What we can conclude from this chapter is that a publisher needs to think in terms of data-led media sell. This is the future of digital advertising. He has to figure out ways to use AI to defend revenue by claiming a higher percentage of the ad-money.

There are a lot of black boxes in the supply chain. A recent study (May 2020) shows that 15% of the ad-money goes to unknown sources in the supply chain. A publisher has to cut through this and deliver value to the marketer. A publisher should consider in-housing of SSP stack to sustain and grow business. The next chapter covers the vast area of bidders and meta DSPs in detail.

Questions

1. What strategy should a publisher adopt for revenue leaks?

2. How does in-housing benefit a publisher?

3. What is AI-led dynamic floor pricing, and how does it help to boost revenues?

Solutions

1. Programmatic is an open market-based ecosystem. Private deals happen, but the design itself is open in nature. The two places where a publisher can fix the revenue leaks and maximize revenue are as follows:

   a. A publisher should have control and view of the primary auctions that are being conducted. This helps to put floor prices efficiently.

   b. A publisher should also try to have a view on the supply chain for the direct demand source and always try to reduce reseller networks. Efficient supply chains will always help in reducing hops and increase revenue.

   Beyond the auction and supply chain, a publisher can also look into curating new content types depending on the audience features.

2. In-housing can help a publisher to gain access to primary auctions, control on supply paths, and seek more effective custom content types. Beyond this, in-housing can also help in implement AI to enhance eCPM by driving different floor prices based on microsegments and dynamic floor prices to counter DSP's bid shading algorithm.

3. The advent of first-price auction prompted DSPs to introduce bid shading algorithm. This enables a DSP to win a bid at the lowest possible price. To counter the DSP AI, namely, bid shading, the primary exchange (conducting the primary auctions) should deploy an AI-generated surge to the floor price. This kind of SSP AI would constantly force the floor prices in the upward direction. A bid shading algorithm saves upwards of over 30% for an advertiser on the media cost. This money is a direct loss for the publisher, and an SSP AI-based surge mechanism can help a publisher regain this revenue – if not all, then at least partly.

CHAPTER 5
Bidders and Meta DSPs

Introduction

In a programmatic ecosystem, an aggregate supply is an easily available commodity. Like any other marketplace, the person or system that is doing the buy needs to have experience and acumen to find the right commodity units.

I would like to compare this with fishery or gain market. In the case of fishery, when the ships come to a dock, they have a catch that is a mix of various things, and the complete stock is just put up for auction. Similarly, when the grain farmer brings their stock to the market, they all have the same product with different quality standards. In both cases, there is a large pile of stock with different ratings of products, and the buyers need to keep an eye to pick out the best available product at a competitive price.

A bidder is a tool that helps the media buyer to buy media programmatically. It is the heart and soul of DSP, which may have many other components.

Traditional methods

Traditionally, digital buying was conducted in a block fashion. In this case, the buyer would approach a publisher and buy either block impressions, for example, 10,000,000 impressions or a block of 1 week, irrespective of the number of impressions it serves.

For obvious reasons, a 1-week buy would internally correspond to some benchmark of impressions. This mechanism gained traction from the mid-1990s. Eventually, the supply and demand aggregators showed up. Programmatic is defined as media trade automation. However, RTB is a more popular format of programmatic. RTB started gaining traction in 2013 when a large percentage of marketers and publishers started trading media using RTB mechanics; soon after, DMPs showed up to enhance the targeting fundamentals of the marketer.

From this book's perspective, I have considered RTB and programmatic synonymously. Any media that can be auctioned in real or near-real time should come under the programmatic bracket. An auction channel or protocol can also support block deals, but that has to be an add-on, and the channel should be limited to only block buys.

Different industry buyers have different KPIs from the media and audience. It takes enormous resources to do effective buys day-on-day. Marketers constantly look to optimize ROI on media and audience. For this reason alone, a marketer goes to great lengths to find the best set of tools and people to perform this function.

In the last 25 years, the ad-tech stack has evolved multiple times. We can see that every 2-3 years new flavors of tools have surfaced. This makes about 10 generations of technologies that a marketer would have seen in his/her career span of 25 years. Today, advanced markets do up to 80% media trading via programmatic, and it is still growing at 25% YoY worldwide. New formats of trading are getting encompassed in the auction format every year. It is an easy, scalable, and dependable format of media and audience trading. The market place is plagued with chronic problems of transparency, brand safety, and frauds. It is an understatement that the marketplace can use big time overhauling.

In-housing of the buy function is seen by many marketers as a mid- to long-term solution. Where in-housing not only addresses the long due problems, it also generates trust and sustainability within the marketer's internal teams. There are many flavors of in-housing, as described by the IAB. I have tried to take up a pure approach where data and tech can be owned by the buyer.

This chapter will help in understanding the "under the hood" working of key systems in the buy function and what a buyer can expect from this gamut of tools and techniques. It further helps to set expectations and how some of these KPIs can be attained.

Structure

- Reference bidding architecture:
    - Retargeting
    - Similar users versus contextual

- o Key performance indicators

- o A typical programmatic campaign structure

- o Using data in media buy

- Bidder:

    - o Supply path optimization

    - o Working of a programmable bidder

    - o AI algorithms in working

    - o Use CRM data for bidding

    - o Creating and activating CRM segments

- Meta DSP:

    - o Laying on top of bidders and networks

    - o CDP – tracking user journey and data activation

    - o Optimization

- Attribution and tracking systems

- How an ad-network works

- Managing brand safety

- Measurement KPIs and techniques

- BOTS

Objective

A buyer today has to decide between the seats of many DSPs. In case he/she wants to engage with in-housing of a DSP, he/she is left with a bigger challenge of build versus buy and so on. This chapter tries to explain the fundamentals of the buy mechanism and the customizations and expectations that one can have from it.

Data-led media buy concepts require a CDP and bidder to work together. I will recommend that the reader runs through the CDP chapter before proceeding further. Secondly, I have explained the RTB protocol in the previous "Exchanges, Ad-Servers, and Header Bidding" chapter and hence will not repeat the text, as this is an important piece that needs to be understood.

I have tried to explain the working of the multi-class classification model's working to optimize for CPM, CPC, and so on. It will be better if the reader has a basic understanding of the model if he/she wants to code. In terms of design, the text should suffice.

This chapter may help the reader with the following:

1. Working of a bidder

2. Various buy **Key Performance Indicators (KPIs)**

3. Meta DSP – an omnichannel approach

4. What it takes to in-house buy function for technology and data ownership

Reference bidding architecture

A bidder is a buy-side engine of a programmatic DSP. In its simplest configuration, a bidder can do the following:

1. Trade media and not the audience (in the current ecosystem)

2. Enable to serve creatives

3. Receive impression and billing confirmations

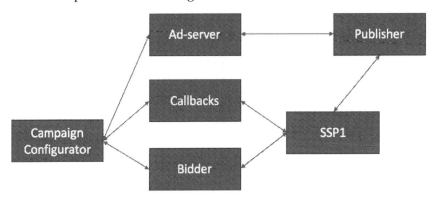

Figure 5.1: High-level view of a DSP

A DSP design is depicted in the preceding figure. The various blocks depicted in *Figure 5.1* are as follows:

1. **SSP1**: A bidder can be attached to many SSPs that will source supply for the buyer. This communication happens via the RTB.

2. **Bidder**: It is an app that does bid responses based on the campaigns that it would hold. Typically, a bidder can respond as **No Bid Request (NBR)** or a bid request that represents the willingness to bid for the media.

3. **Callback**: It is an app that caters for information about impressions and wins bids. In the case of post-auction, if the bidder's bid wins the exchange, then it notifies the bidder callback via nurl and burl.

a. **Win bids**: Every time a bidder wins an auction, the exchange fires a signal to acknowledge that the bidder has won the bid. This signal is referred to as a win bid. To make this happen, the bidder gives a call back URL in the nurl parameter in the bid response. The exchange gives an http call to this URL for this signal acknowledgment. From a business perspective, it can be constituted that the impression has been served.

b. **Billable impression**: During the time of the auction if the impression served is considered to be billable, then the exchange fires the signal to acknowledge that the impression is billable. This is done by using the burl parameter in the bid request. Similar to the win bid call, the burl is also fired by exchange via an http protocol to the bidder callback module.

4. **Ad-server**: Helps in handling the creatives and its rendering. Its detailed explanation has been given in the earlier chapters.

5. **Campaign configurator**: This module manages the campaign configuration. These usually consist of four blocks in which campaign KPIs are defined. They are as follows:

a. **Insertion order (IO)** represents the mandate of a KPI for media buy. It typically has a budget, generic, and/or specific expectation of the media buy and some information of target segments. IO is usually the output of media planning.

b. The campaign is an execution block of an IO. An IO is usually broken down into multiple campaigns. This is usually done post-breaking down of the mandate to execution blocks by allocating some budgets and so on.

c. A strategy is a logical block within a campaign. Programmatic enables a high degree of targeting. The targeting is achieved by creating segments that can be audience- or media-based. Media-based segments are usually referred to as contextual. Each of these segments targeting encompasses different media buy rules, CPM, and budget.

d. Campaign configurators usually interact with the callback module to get the impression counts and billing data. Billing data is crucial to update budgets on strategy, campaign, and IO level.

e. **Creatives**: Campaign creatives are loaded in the ad-server for further use. Typically, on the bid win, when the control is passed onto the publisher along with the creative details. The publisher side of the system can then pull the creative and required scripts for rendering.

For obvious reasons, a bidder is usually connected with multiple SSPs or supply sources. This design ensures that the bidder always stays with adequate media.

> **Note: RTB and ad-server work hand-in-hand. RTB enables the trading of media, and the ad-server helps in delivering of media/creative. This modular architecture helps in getting new formats of creative into RTB rather quickly. Another way to look at this is, if the media wants to trade programmatically, they need to start from making the ad-server talk using RTB mechanics.**

Today's buy mechanics heavily depend on audience play. This requires a CDP to be attached to a bidder assuming that our CDP is also handling the data activation part. This is depicted in the following figure:

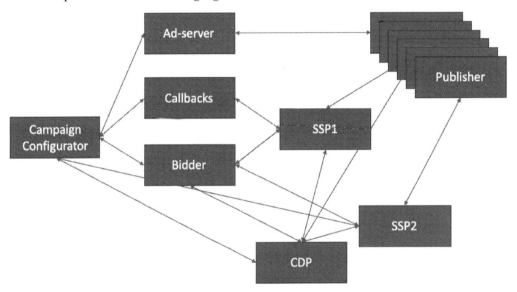

Figure 5.2: High-level view of the programmatic ecosystem

The addition of CDP enables the following:

1. To perform audience-based targeting and ad-serving.

2. The campaign manager views audience-based segments. This helps is doing a degree in media planning.

3. Audience-based targeting enables a key feature of creative/strategy/campaign-based user frequency capping. This means that if a user has seen a creative for x number of times in y number of duration, then the user is shifted in the outlier bucket and is not targeted any more.

The CDP usually manages the ID syncs and maps between various components in the ecosystem. Essentially, there are three points where the user needs to be tracked:

1. Publisher site
2. Exchange
3. Bidder

Tracking the users across sites is a work of CDP/DMP. In certain cases such as sync, it is also done by the bidder and exchange. These mechanisms have been explained in the previous chapters.

Another aspect of data-led buy is for the marketer to use first-party data. A CRM or an equivalent is usually a source for the marketer. This is shown in the following figure:

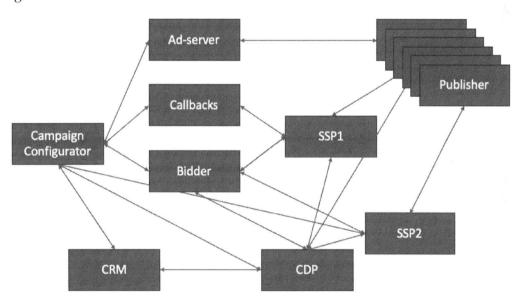

Figure 5.3: *High-level view of the programmatic ecosystem*

A CRM usually stores data of invoices, subscribers, and so on. This data can be used to create lookalikes for prospecting. Also, these segments can be used for cross-selling/up-selling and/or enhanced content/service consumption. This is done via retargeting.

Retargeting

Retargeting is a process where the user is tracked across media for a specific KPI. From a user perspective, it looks as if he/she sees the same ad over and over again across publishers.

Retargeting is an important part of the programmatic performance. One of the iconic use cases of retargeting is – abandoned cart. In one of the first pressing scenarios, it was noted by online retailers that when a user abandoned the cart (where the user shops and fills the online cart and then before paying just quits the site), there was a high degree of chances that, if the user was reminded, then the user would come back and make the purchase.

Eventually, many use cases came up using a similar concept. Some of them are as follows:

1. **Cross-selling**: When the marketer wants to sell other products to the same user.

2. **Reminder**: Similar to abandon cart use case where a user is reminded for renewal and so on.

3. **Intend capture**: Once the intent to make a purchase is established, then the marketer would want to have brand visibility.

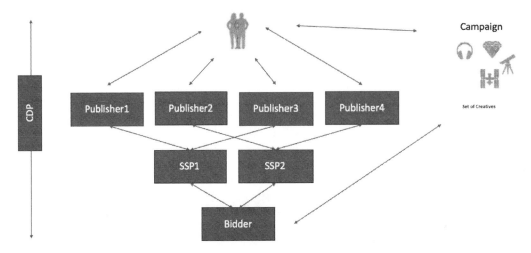

Figure 5.4: The retargeting scenario

The preceding figure shows the working of retargeting. This is as follows:

1. A user is tracked within various publishers. This is usually done using third-party cookies for user tracking and ad-serving.

2. The bidder is given a campaign KPI of retargeting along with creatives and a set of targeted users.

Beyond that, it is just a regular working of a programmatic campaign as described in the text earlier.

Similar users versus contextual

Similar users are also known as lookalikes, and contextual-based targeting is very similar. This is further detailed out in the following table:

Similar users	Contextual
Assigns a segment to a user.	Assigns a segment to the media.
Uses a reference set of users to extrapolate similar characteristics of users and finally forming a user set/segment.	Uses keywords, content category, and so on to relate the content to campaign KPI relation.
Can use AI/ML to create similar user segments.	Can use AI/ML to create a context of media.
Usually uses media and audience features in the AI/ML algorithms.	Uses media-based features in the AI/ML algorithms.

Table 5.1: *Lookalikes based on audiences versus content*

As the working of a similar audience and contextual targeting is similar, the AI/ML working is similar in both scenarios.

Key performance indicators – KPIs

Unlike sell functions in which there are limited KPIs such as eCPM, fill, and impressions, the buy functions can have a whole lot of KPIs. However, we can easily break this down at four levels:

1. **Cost Per Mille (CPM)**

2. **Cost Per Click (CPC)**

3. **Cost Per Acquisition (CPA)**

4. **Cost Per View/Visit (CPV)**

There are other KPIs that have come up such as **Cost Per Sales** (**CPS**), **Cost Per Install** (**CPI**), and so on. However, from a programmatic perspective, it is only these four kinds of flows that exist, so even if one comes up with something different, then that would lie in one of them.

Before getting into the KPI definition of the above, one thing that needs to be understood is that the KPI usually stems from the way the execution can be quantified. For example, footfall is a brand recall-based KPI that is similar to unique user reach, which is similar to CPM KPI.

The definitions of the KPIs are as follows:

- CPM is a cost per 1,000 impressions. There is a complementing metric on top of this, which is viewability.

- CPC is a cost per click. This is one of the most common KPI for a native format.

- CPA is a cost per acquisition. This usually entails an external callback to register the acquisition. The acquisition can also be hybrid. For example, user registration plus first transaction or user registration and two logins in 7 days.

- CPV is a cost per view and is usually used for the video and/or VAST. This includes various quartiles and so on. For example, first 10-sec view, half view, 90% view, or full view.

A typical programmatic campaign structure

A campaign designed for programmatic usually has the following features:

1. Campaign-level features.

2. Strategy level where the strategy to a campaign is many-to-one relation.

It is safe to visualize that the strategy is the actual entity that bids for the bid request.

The campaign usually holds the following features:

1. Budget

2. Campaign reference details

3. Flight

4. Goal – CPM, CPC, CPA, and so on.

5. Tracking pixels

6. PMP that can be targeted for the campaign

The strategy usually holds the following features:

1. Budget at the strategy level.

2. Pacing – ASAP, even, and so on.

3. Goal – usually, this is the same as the campaign goals.

4. Tracking pixels – this will supersede the campaign tracking pixels.

5. PMP.

6. Audience segment for targeting or blacklisting.

7. Domain, ad-unit, or publisher whitelisting or blacklisting.

It is safe to say that every DSP chooses a campaign structure of its choice. The preceding structure is being used by numerous DSPs that I have used, and it makes sense because it is designed to use the RTB-defined trading mechanics.

Some DSPs support the budget-level aggregation at the IO level. This makes IO campaign a one-to-many relationship. The idea to manage a marketing mandate at the IO level makes the campaign to be handled simply by giving space to create multiples of them. However, this also creates a challenge that the bidder usually will not be able to handle while competing strategies of different campaigns.

Note: It is safe to say that the bidding is done on a per strategy basis. There is always a chance that two strategies of the same campaign completes with each other. This will increase the cost of media and audience for the advertiser. Hence, a campaign needs to be configured keeping such things in view. This complexity increases if the operator has to check all the details till the IO level and until all campaigns are connected via IO.

I suggest keeping a KPI consolidated to one campaign per platform and media source. This will keep things manageable and efficient so that there is a trade-off between ease and efficiency.

Using data in media buy

There are usually two distinct ways to use data in media buy. They are as follows:

1. **Outliers**: The user base that we need to avoid at the campaign or bidder level.

2. **Target**: The user base that we need to target at the strategy or campaign level.

Bidder

A bidder is an engine that does the media buying, as explained in *Figure 5.1*. A bidder is directly connected to the exchange via the RTB. The flow may look as follows:

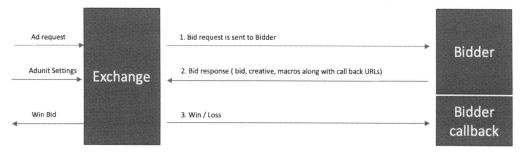

Figure 5.5: *Exchange to bidder - sequence diagram*

The flow runs as follows:

1. The exchange fires a bid request toward the bidder. The bidder behaves like an http-based RTB server and responds.

2. The response is in the same http session and is referred to as bid response.

3. The exchange further conducts an auction and informs the bidder if the bid is won or lost in the auction. This is usually referred to as a callback.

A bidder may end up receiving bid requests from multiple exchanges and hence needs to maintain complex request management mechanics.

Note: A bidder usually needs to respond within 250 ms. This is including the usual network latency of 200 ms. The exchange integration with the bidder usually starts with a ping test, which allows to position bidders in the same geographic zone, to minimize network latency.

Supply path optimization

The advent of header bidding mechanics makes multiple paths for the same inventory to reach the bidder. The mechanics have been explained in detail in the previous chapter. So, two scenarios arise from this:

1. A bidder may end up bidding for the same space multiple times. This may lead to internal competition between a single strategy with multiple instances of the same media.

2. A bidder may choose a supply path without realizing that the supply may be available at another path at a cheaper price and perhaps better metadata.

In both scenarios, it becomes imperative for the bidder to apply supply path optimization techniques at the bidder level. This makes the working of the SPO different because all other optimizations, that is, CPM, CPC, CPA, and CPV, work at a campaign level.

The supply and its path can be defined with the following attributes:

`Adunit | Publisher | Exchange1 | exchange2 |Bidder`

An in-house bidder will be able to manage an SPO at the most granular level, with exuberant exceptional handling. In case you are using a standard DSP, then you may choose to blacklist at the exchange level.

Note: Ad-unit, Tag-Id, and ad-space are usually used interchangeably, where ad-unit is more from the publisher aspect, and tag-Id is an RTB variable.

Bidder reference design

A typical bidder entails a set of filters and AI algorithms that help it to buy media efficiently. Essentially, there are three folds to this:

1. The first fold helps filter out the bot, outliers, SPO, and so on. This usually works at the bidder level. If the bid request is an outlier, bot, fraud, and so on, then the request is dropped at this level itself.

2. The second fold is the filtering process at the campaign and strategy level. This is where the demand is found for the relevant supply. If a relevant campaign or strategy does not exist for the bid request, the request is dropped.

3. The third level is the AI layer that determines the price or drop for the request.

This can be further broken down. The following are the steps of execution of a bidder function:

1. **SPO:** A bidder usually deploys supply path optimization. This helps to do the first-level filter of the bid stream.

2. The second level of filtering is done for the availability of the budget and creatives. Availability of creatives is one of the big factors for NBR.

3. The filter step consists of filtering against various parameters:

    a. Black/whitelisting of domains, ad-units, and IP addresses.

    b. Filtering against OS, device, display type, carrier, location, and so on.

    c. Filtering against publisher- or audience-level attributes.

    d. Filtering against black/whitelist audience list. This is typically referred to as audience-level targeting.

4. The fourth level is where the AI/ML kicks in and starts to score the audience and media.

5. If the control flow has reached the last step, then it means the only decision left to decide is the price of the bid. The prerequisite to take this decision is as follows:

    a. The bidder has a campaign and strategy that qualifies for the bid request.

    b. The audience and media clear the required audience and media quality standards.

    c. The bid request qualifies for the audience.

At this point, the AI/ML jumps in to ascertain the right price to win.

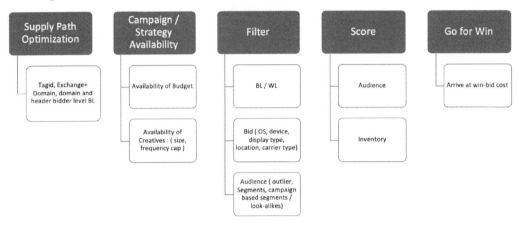

Figure 5.6: Internal bidder control flow

Two aspects that need to be taken care of in terms of load and diversity of load are as follows:

1. A large DSP could receive TPS to the tune of a few million.

2. The large DSP could receive demand from various geo.

This means that the bidder has to be scalable at the geo and within-geo level. This would look as follows:

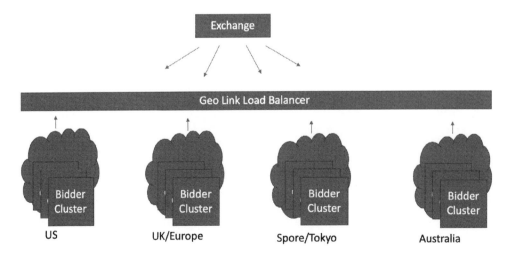

Figure 5.7: Programmable bidder flow

The functionality, complexity, and scale make DSP development a daunting task. Perhaps, the technical architecture of the DSP and exchange demands another level of skillset altogether.

As a decision maker or in-housing from the brand side, it is a good idea to bring in experts to handle this side of the technicality.

Working of a programmable bidder

A programmable bidder typically has one feature beyond a regular bidder, as stated previously. A programmable bidder allows the operator to choose the algorithm along with the campaign and data. The addition of loadable algorithms can provide many benefits to the media buyer.

Note: As of July 2020, I have not come across any company that has deployed a programmable bidder for a large-scale media buy process.

The need for a programmable bidder comes when the buyer has time-critical buys that need to be done at scale. This becomes critical to an extent that he/she is ready to do an A/B test on buys itself to reach a mature optimize level quickly.

The ability to use custom algorithms arises when the generic "out-of-the-box" algorithms come along with the DSP. One may argue that such a situation never arises. I think that every business is unique in its timing, customer connect, approach, and/or product/service line; if one believes this to be true, then how is it that a set of four or five algorithms fix the entire universe of brands? When brands start to look at the data, the next step will be to look at the custom buy algorithms. With the advent of data-led media buy, which is not a time far from today when brands would lease algorithms for media buy.

In both the scenarios of custom and multiple custom algorithms, one needs the bidder capable of hot deploying the algorithm code.

In addition to the hot deployment feature, a custom algorithm needs a sandbox environment to efficiently build a generic algorithm.

A programmable bidder architecture may look like as follows:

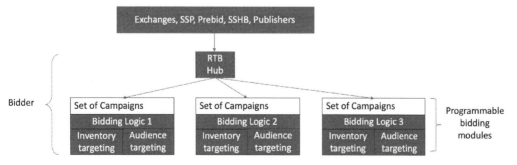

Figure 5.8: High-level view of a programmable bidder

Beyond RTB handling, the programmable bidder design is fairly different. In a programmable bidder, the operator can choose to work with a set of algorithms.

A programmable bidder allows two scenarios:

1. Exposes a library of algorithms to be used

2. Allows uploading custom algorithms that would facilitate the buy

Such a design allows us to reach an optimal buy level much more efficiently. With this kind of deployment, a complex set of KPIs can be targeted with much more ease.

All in all, a programmable bidder is the nirvana of a programmatic buy ecosystem.

AI algorithms in working

Essentially, there are two questions that the optimization techniques provide an answer to. They are as follows:

1. Should I bid or not?

2. At what price do I need to bid?

Question 1 usually covers the CPM scenarios. Question 2 covers CPS, CPA, CPS, CPI, and so on. The approach can be generic at the start, however, with the incorporation of new data more complex and apt treatment can be introduced.

> **Note: There are many bidding strategies that are employed by the DSPs. It can range between high bid costs to cover more precise media to low bid costs to cover more ground. Of course, there are many versions that will be between these two scenarios.**

One of the bidders I am deeply familiar with consists of uses of the "Multi-class classification model." It is a neural net plus logistic regression model that helps in CPM, CPC, CPA, CPI, CPS, and many other kinds of KPI.

It is a fourth-generation model and handles many limitations that others do not. I will try to run an example while explaining the working of these mechanics.

Let us begin with the step-by-step process:

Step1: Need to make a bid with manageable limited numbers.

Let us put it more simply; the RTB allows us to use eight decimal numbers for bidding. Effectively, this makes 10^8 possibilities between a 1 USD bid and 2 USD bid. So, in this case, the bid ranges between 1 C and 10 USD; this will be 10^9 possible values.

Such a large range of numbers is not possible to compute; hence, we need to create blocks. These blocks incorporate the bidding number range (let us call them bins).

This gives three characteristics to a bin:

1. Mix value

2. Max value

3. Number represented

To carry outbidding, we need to fix the number of bins. Let us say we create 50 bins. This largely says that the bidder can bid 50 possible values.

Note: If you are from a publishing background, then think of this like the counter for the line item-based pricing mechanics of DFP. It is similar mechanics.

Step2: Feature-wise data preparation.

In a bidder, there are three sets of features that can be used.:

Sample media features:

1. adInventory Id – also referred to as TagId

2. Exchange Id

3. Application category

4. Application name

5. Site category

6. Site name

7. Position

8. Height

9. Width

10. Bid floor

11. Currency

Sample audience features:

1. User identification type

2. Carrier

3. Connection type

4. Make

5. Model

6. OS

7. Device type

8. Country

9. State

10. City

Sample metric features:

1. Bids

2. No bids

3. Lost bids

4. Impressions

5. Clicks

6. Average CPM

7. Average CPM cost

8. Win rate

9. CTR

10. eCPC

Knowing features from the campaign KPI perspective and ensuring that it participates in the model is essential for the model to work.

The next thing is to do feature hashing. This is where the number game starts. Feature hashing essentially has three steps:

1. Ascertain the variable type of the feature. A variable type defines the treatment of a variable in the model.

2. Estimate the possible values of the feature.

3. Fix a hash scale of the feature.

A sample of feature hashing planning based on the few variables is as follows:

Feature class	Feature name	Feature type	Feature unique	Feature hashes
Inventory	adInventory	Categorial	145	256
Inventory	Bid Floor	Number	0	0
Audience	City	Categorial	20,990	4,096

Table 5.2: Type of variables

The feature hashes are in order of 2^x.

Step3: Using an autoencoder for neural network-based learning.

Say, for example, a set of 100k unique features gets translated into 2^15 feature hashes or 32,768 features. This kind of hashing is possible, and it is possible to reconstruct the original value from the features.

The concept states that if a multidimensional number (vector) can be reduced and then again reconstructed, then based on the correlation of dimensions, the vector can retain the knowledge.

This process needs to take care of two aspects:

1. It needs to ensure that the knowledge remains to reconstruct the original vector.

2. It ensures that if some new input comes, then it can be catered, and the knowledge should not be limited to the training data. This problem is also called overfitting.

In general, the problem of overfitting can be resolved by introducing randomness, which is an easier way to increase the sample size. This will introduce border cases from the real world.

> **Note: Let us say you make a training set with 10% of the production data. Assume that the 10% sample had skews in the user behavior. Now, the model got trained to a level that it can only deal with the data that is similar to training set and does not perform with other kind of scenarios.**
>
> **This problem can be resolved by giving enough randomness to the sample data.**

A graphical representation of this process is shown in *Figure 5.9*.

Essentially, the model is trying to learn by reducing the xn to h-h2 to exn (xn and e represent the error).

The figure itself is a two-dimensional representation of a multidimensional number. The x, h, and ex are multidimensional numbers or simply put – a vector.

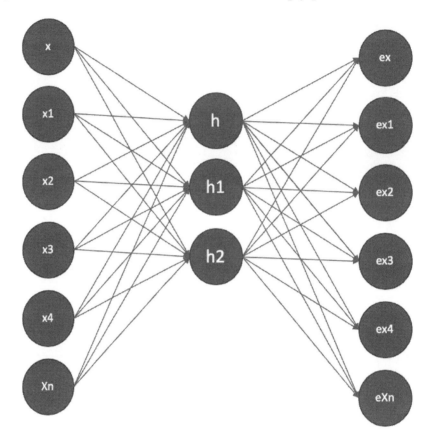

Figure 5.9: Working of vectors in a neural network

Think of it like this – in the x, y graph, a point is represented by (x,y). So, in a two-dimensional number schematic, a number is x,y – hence, in an n-dimensional number schematic, a number will be x, x1, x2 -> xn. This case implies on all three levels. This is the reason that every number in the dimension is connected to every other number.

Now, it is possible to reduce an n-dimensional number to a lower-dimensional number. This process is called dimensional reduction.

However, to ensure that the dimensional reduction is done properly, we again rebuild the vector. This time we see that the rebuilt vector has some errors (which is represented by e in *Figure 5.9*).

An autoencoder model requires to be retrained multiple times to reduce this error and form a correct h vector that represents the learning.

In the RTB stream and the win bid logs, we get data to create the preceding model. This requires a few more steps. They are as follows:

Step 4: Sampling and training.

This essentially means that eXn is a bin vector. However, now every dimension also needs to represent a bid value. This is ascertained in Step1.

As every dimension is connected, it means that every feature is connected to every bin. This also means that every bid request is connected to every bin. Every bin gives a probability to every bid request to win.

Let us construct the exact model that will exactly get built for training. First, we need to understand the core data. This is represented in the following table:

Use case	Metric	Number
Assumption – Total number of bids	Number	1,000
Total wins %	Percentage	10
Total loss %	Percentage	90
Want to win	Percentage	1,000

Table 5.3: Sample training data summary

The second thing we require is bin buckets. This can be seen in the following table:

Bin bucket label	Min (USD)	Max (USD)
Bin 1	0.1	0.5
Bin 2	0.5001	1
Bin 3	1.0001	1.5
Bin 4	1.5001	2
Bin 5	2.0001	2.5

Table 5.4: Bin allocation for bid price

In a real-life scenario, you may want to create up to 50 bins. Every bin is a possible bid value. One needs to be careful about the compute and memory factor when arriving at this number. For now, let us say that we have 50 bins.

The third thing we need is sampling mechanics.

Let us pick up data from *Table 5.3* and proceed:

Win – 10% ->that translates to-> 100

Loss – 90% -> that translates to-> 900

The distribution of 1:9 is critical in the latter part of the compute.

Now, we need to allocate wins and losses to the 100 wins. This is the way we tell the system what it needs to do. Hence, using the distribution factor we proceed:

Win-win - > 10 % translates to 10 bids-> reduction by 5% of the bid value ->may end up getting into lower bin allocation-> for win.

Win-loss -> 90 % translates to 90 bids-> reduction by 5% of the bid value -> may end up getting in lower bin -> for loss.

We try to teach the AI that by reducing the bid value by 5–90% of bids may lose and 10% of bids could win.

We do a similar formula to the loss bids:

Loss-loss – > 90 % translates to 810 ->increase the bid value by 5% -> may end up getting into the higher bid bucket.

Loss-win –> 10% translates to 90> increase the bid value by 5% -> may end up getting into the higher bid bucket.

So, now we have all the building blocks for the model to run.

Let's recap and summarize this. The model plan phase would include:
1. Defining feature hash for the bid request.
2. Defining bins.
3. Define dimension reduction.
4. Plan a training strategy.

The stepwise run would look as follows:
1. Hashing
2. Dimension reduction
3. Bin setup for a probabilistic score

All of the preceding is to create a model. The second part is the bidder implementation. The process looks the same with only one difference. The process along with the difference is mentioned as follows:
1. Bid request
2. Hashing
3. Dimension reduction
4. Bid probabilistic score on a bed request basis using sigmoid
5. Go for the bid

The 4 steps in the model creation are used for repetitive training, but in the case of the bidder, this is used for deriving the bid price.

The CPC, CPA, CPI, and so on processes work out similarly from the model perspective. From the KPI attainment perspective, the input and outcome vary a lot. The differences are as follows:

1. The data universe changes – the conversion data (features) are included.

2. Now only one bin is needed.

Once the click, acquisition, or install data is included, the model trains itself. The features of them could be as follows:

1. Click Id

2. Campaign name

3. Install Id

4. Creative Id

5. Bid Id

The probability factor suggests if the bidder should go for the win.

From the bidder perspective, the flow looks as follows:

1. The CPC, CPA, CPI, and so on goals make the bidder decide if the bidder should bid.

2. In the case of CPM or if step1 is yes – the bidder decides at what price should the bidder go for a win.

Note: The first part of the model can be enabled by the CDP. The second part needs to be embedded into the bidder. This kind of a working makes the CDP and bidder tightly coupled.

Other regression models are deployed by the bidder. But, they usually do not cover loss scenarios.

Bidders also deploy collaborative mechanics to generate lookalikes for CPC, CPI, CPA, and so on. This is a good technique. However, unsupervised algorithms will always have limitations.

A neural network is a good solution. One can even choose to build graph-based models. As of now, I am not aware of any bidder using graphs or networks to bid assistance. However, this is an area that has immense possibilities.

From an architectural perspective, a bidder and the AI/ML should have loose coupling for frequent upgrades. Also, as explained in earlier chapters, this kind of algorithm implementation could have a significant bearing on the CDP data strategy and implementation.

Use CRM data for bidding

CRM data is the deterministic data that provides critical data metric for all performance KPIs.

There are many ways to compute and predict user behavior using deterministic data in conjunction with the intended data. With the user's privacy on formation/rise, CRM data can be used for analyses for advertising usage.

CRM data consists of typically acquired users. Some of the characteristics of such data are as follows:

1. Whenever these users are on the advertiser's website, they usually do a sign in or are assigned a persistent ID. This ID can be used to track the user via "Audience Extension." This means that tracking an already acquired user is simpler than tracking a prospect.

2. Once we can determine the behavior of the "acquired user," a prospect is just an extrapolation of that acquired user. This is usually referred to as a lookalike. Lookalike is a CDP use case and is explained in that earlier chapter.

3. An acquired user, depending on his/her brand loyalty attributes, brand experience, and products on offer is the best candidate for cross-sell/up-sell.

Using customer data that directly links to PII from a marketing perspective has a lot of legal aspects. The best way to deal with that is to take user consent. There is a good chance that the consent has been acquired as a blanket while acquiring the user from a service level. I usually recommend that the consent should be taken at a cookie ID formation level.

> **Note: Audience extension is a case where a user can be tracked within multiple exchanges and publishers, whereas from an advertiser's perspective, this seems to be straightforward. However, a retailer who owns supply and demand needs to look into a DSP format to manage their users on other publishers.**

There is no supreme answer in this case of managing consent effectively, but I find this one particular flow to work and answer most of the questions. The flow is described in the following figure:

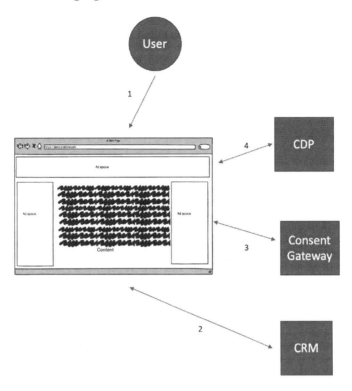

Figure 5.10: *User consent control flow*

The figure can be explained as follows:

1. User visits the site of the advertiser.

2. The site queries the CRM to pull all the relevant details.

3. The consent gateway ensures that the data we are about to use for marketing has the relevant permission.

4. The data is then passed into the CDP.

All this has to happen in the same user session to be relevant.

Creating and activating CRM segments

CRM data consists of many user and product attributes. There are few principles on which CRM segments are created. They are as follows:

1. Address existing users in terms of products and services that they used or subscribed to.

2. Create a map of products and services that are correlated in terms of features, tenure, and prices.

The preceding two principles help us create the following use cases:

1. In the case of existing customers, we can target them for cross-selling and up-sell.

2. We can create lookalike segment by using existing user data to create a larger lookalike segment for prospecting.

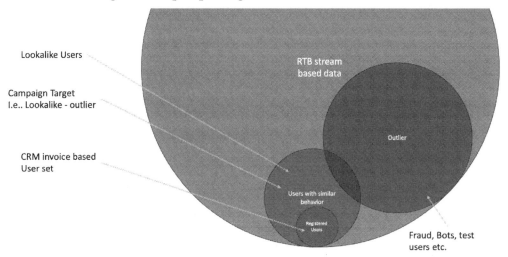

Figure 5.11: *Data universe and AI-based segments*

The details of *Figure 5.11* are as follows:

1. The RTB stream data becomes a data universe.

2. The registered users-based segment is created using the CRM data.

3. A lookalike segment is created using the segment: CRM-Registered users.

4. As a general practice, we strike out the outliers.

In an in-house bidder scenario, we just need to sync the data to make the targeted ad-serving possible. The only drop happens on the exchange's end, that is, if the user is not available on the exchange's publishers.

Using CRM data for targeted ad-serving is one of the biggest advantages that in-housing brings.

Note: Prospecting is a case where a new user is targeted for a particular product or service. "A prospect" user is a potential user.

Meta DSP

A meta-DSP, in the easiest terms is an aggregate of the DSP. The key components of a DSP are campaign configuration and bidder/media buy engine. It becomes essential that a meta-DSP can manage a central campaign theme across all the engines.

As explained in *Figure 5.10*, there are four components in a bidder. They are as follows:

1. Campaign configuration

2. Ad-server

3. Call backs

4. Bidder

A meta-DSP needs to have the campaign configuration module with it. Apart from that, a meta-DSP may keep an ad-serving and callback module depending on the guest platform.

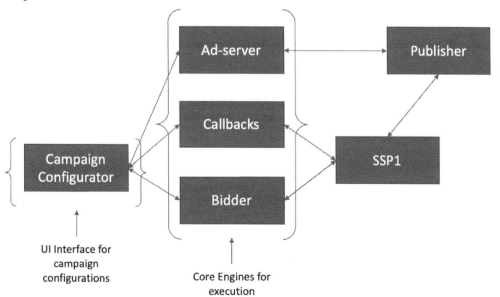

Figure 5.12: High-level view of a DSP

This concept and the decoupled design of the meta-DSP allows many possible configurations. A typical meta-DSP's high-level design could look as described in the preceding figure.

Laying on top of bidders and networks

A meta-DSP gives a much larger view of media buy and can execute a larger part of the media plan because it connects with other platform engines and gives a consolidated and wider view of media. In agency circuits, a meta-DSP is usually referred as an ATD, that is, agency trading desk.

This becomes the central theme of the meta-DSP, and it relentlessly tries to get other platforms to connect to it.

This also means that a bidder or ad-network that needs to participate in a meta-DSP framework has to support some kind of a microservice architecture along with data transfer mechanics for central reporting.

This requires the campaign structure to be very dynamic because every new platform could have a different campaign or creative structure. Secondly, such systems eventually need to work using naming conventions to communicate between different guest platforms.

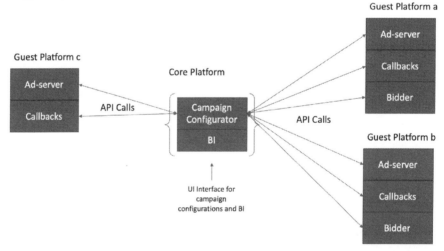

Figure 5.13: *High-level view of a meta-DSP*

The preceding figure showcases the following:

1. Guest platform a and Guest platform b are RTB-based platforms that are connected with the meta-DSP.

2. Guest platform c is an ad-network.

3. As the name suggests, the guest platforms are not owned by the meta-DSP. They would usually come up as partners. There could be many commercial arrangements between them.

4. Core platform is the heart of the meta-DSP, which manages campaign configurations and reports/dashboards.

CDP – tracking user journey and data activation

Due to the mere structure of the meta-DSP, a CDP becomes very challenging and also necessary.

Where a CDP, from an audience activation perspective in a DSP, only needs to sync with exchange and because the ad-serving gets done on the DSP's ID mechanics, the rest of the user syncing is not typically required.

In the case of a meta-DSP, a CDP has the following work:

1. Track users with all the guest platforms via impression, click, and conversing calls

2. Manage user frequency

3. Create target segments

4. Activate the data via sync on guest platforms

This has been described in the following figure:

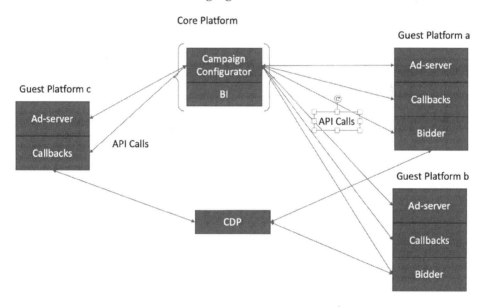

Figure 5.14: *Workflow of CDP in a meta-DSP*

As a meta-DSP is very much dependent on the underlying guest platforms, a CDP needs to be able to manage various mechanics for syncs and exports.

Optimization

Every platform offers generic features for filters as follows:

1. Target options:
   a. Geo
   b. IP address
   c. Browser and so on
2. User frequency cap
3. Segment-based targeting
4. Blacklisting and whitelisting

Once these features are mapped to the core platform's CDP, a CDP can then use an AI layer to suggest filters to be implemented in the guest platforms. It could be strange that different platforms could be giving different datasets and the CDP may end up suggesting contradictory suggestions for the same campaign in different guest platforms.

If a meta-DSP works with, say 50 guest platforms, then this kind of system becomes a necessity.

All these factors make the development and maintenance of a meta-DSP a daunting exercise.

Attribution and tracking systems

Usually, attribution and tracking systems are two different services. As they sit on the same dataset and in-housing does not follow Google's paradigm, these two things can be looked at as one.

The following figure tries to give an integrated view on tracking and attribution.

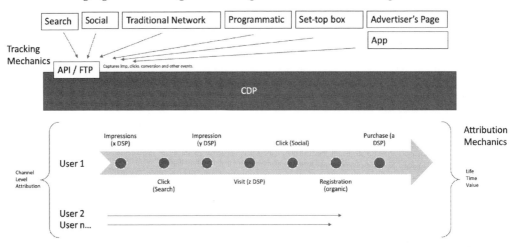

***Figure 5.15**: User tracking in a meta-DSP*

Tracking is a critical part of the attribution. Tracking is essentially data collections. There are three things that one needs to track:

1. **Campaign**: Impressions
2. **Campaign**: Clicks
3. **Campaign**: Conversions

The second set of attributes that needs to track are as follows:

1. **Campaign**: Platform
2. **Campaign**: Timeline

Once the data is into the system, the tracking part is complete.

The second part is a state engine that is used to create a trail for all KPI attainments.

As shown in the preceding figure, for User 1, User 2, to User n, who had done purchases, the state engine maintains all the channels that helped in the final acquisition. This mechanic is called **attribution**.

One of the most important parts of the acquired user is the lifetime value that the user generates on account of the product or service for that brand. A state engine can suggest the channels or the combinations of the channels that should be used to deliver the best-case acquisition scenarios.

How an ad-network works

An ad-network is a closed-loop supply and demand system. An ad-network typically ties up with supply sources and gets direct demand for the said supply. A lot of times an ad-network will rely on indigenous creative formats.

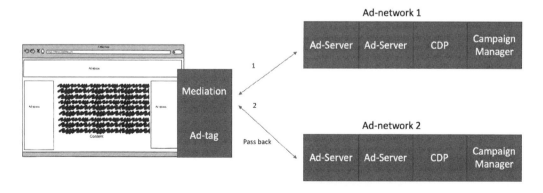

Figure 5.16: High-level view of an ad-network

Mediation plays an important role in an ad-network. As the ad-request is done sequentially, a system is required to manage the control flow in case the fill does not happen in the ad-request.

Figure 5.16 depicts the working of an ad-network.

1. A mediation system can be a client- or server-side implementation. The figure depicts a client-side implementation.

2. The publisher sends the first ad-request to Ad-network1.

3. As Ad-network1 cannot do the fill, there is a pass back. The second ad-network in the configuration is Ad-network2 – hence, the ad-request is passed on it.

Note: As the rendering has to be done within 800 ms (which is an acceptable norm) and one request takes up to 250 ms and the request now has to be done sequentially, a mediation-based system can only allow up to 3 to 5 pass backs.

As the mediation is not auction-based, every level of the mediation needs to keep a floor price to manage demand. This also means that the later level ad-network, even if it has demand, could end up not getting the ad-request itself.

Today, every large publisher and/or advertiser wants to create an ad-network that is usually designed to work in a silo. This is a very wrong approach.

An ad-network, by design, has few issues, which are as follows:

- **Scale**: An ad-network always has scale problems.

- **Performance**: An ad-network for publishers will always fetch sub-optimal revenue due to performance issues.

- An ad-network, beyond a threshold, can become very high maintenance.

Mediation is explained in earlier chapters in greater details.

Managing brand safety

In today's world, where content is distributed via multiple channels and generated in multiple flavors and so on, it becomes obvious that the context of an advertisement and content do not agree with each other.

For example:

1. One does not advertise an energy drink within a piece of flood news.

2. One does not advertise baby products within an adult movie.

Many instances do not work. This is a very serious problem that needs a lot of work from the publisher and advertiser side to make this work.

For starters, there are over 150 IAB content categories and over 5,000 categories that are commonly used by DMPs and CDPs alike. An ideal solution should have the following characteristics:

1. Tag every content with adequate multiple categories.

2. Populate the bid request with all the data.

3. Bidders should host campaigns with relevant categories.

4. Bidder should have a context filter to match campaign context to media context.

Almost all of the preceding is not present in today's ecosystem. Very few companies and start-ups have chosen to pick this problem set.

Anyways, looking at the Google ecosystem, I can comment on the minimal changes that it would take to make this work:

1. **Tagging the content:**
    a. In today's world where the keywords are not tagged properly, it sounds rather unreasonable to expect the publisher to tag all the content.

    b. The answer could be an NLP engine that reads the content and generates the tags in sync with the RTB metadata.

2. **RTB bid request:**
    a. A lot of exchanges do not support the RTB input, and they take the appropriate publisher, content, and site data from the publisher. Beyond this, the few exchanges that take the RTB input may choose to rip all the data beyond the few set parameters.

    b. We need an exchange that will take the RTB as an input and will not rip the packet.

3. **The bidder's filter:**
    a. Most of the bidders work on very select filters. A content-based context is a complete miss.

    b. We need to have dynamic filter mechanics in the bidder so that media-based segments and context-based filters can be attained.

Brand safety in programmatic is a complex issue and needs an overhaul at each point for this to work.

Note: An advertiser needs to see that the bidder can handle such features so that when the apt supply is available. then the bidder should be able to perform these functions.

Measurement KPIs and techniques

Beyond CPM-, CPC-, and CPA-based KPI, which are very direct campaign-related KPI, there are other bidders and media-related KPIs that are used in programmatic. Essentially, the direct KPIs in programmatic are only CPM and CPC because the bidder can only work in those blocks. However, marketing as a whole can have many metrics.

The second way to look at business KPI is the attribution mechanics given metrics. Attribution comes into play in the following blocks ,as depicted in the following figure:

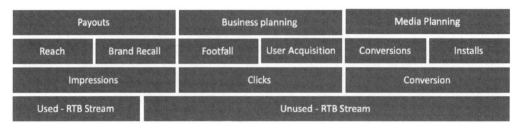

Figure 5.17: High-level measurement metrics

1. Business KPI is used for payouts. For example, post-view, post-click, footfall, conversions, and so on.

2. Attribution can drive secondary metrics that contribute to business KPIs such as user lifetime value, brand recall, reach, and so on.

3. The platform-level attributions consist of impressions, clicks, and a third-level goal (usually acquisition, install, and so on).

In the case of an e-retailer who is a publisher and an advertiser, an apt attribution and rating model become far more complicated.

A retailer looks at its indigenous constant supply and usually limits himself/herself with the inventory he/she has. Ideally, an e-retailer should think in two folds.

Firstly, from the perspective of an advertiser, he/she buys media to sell his/her products.

Secondly, he can use his media to run campaigns for other advertisers. At this point, one would like to think in eCPM terms.

Anyways, one needs to have an understanding of all the blocks to make monitoring metric. I always suggest having a bottom-up approach while keeping business goals in mind.

BOTS

Media frauds are one of the most controversial areas in the programmatic industry. One of the prime components of fraud is the BOTs. Not all BOTS are bad, and some do have genuine uses. For example, a search engine usually deploys a BOT crawler that visits all available sites on the Internet and uses the data to index and optimizes the search.

IAB/ABC maintains a list of qualified browsers and another list of qualified BOTS. Usually, a non-mischievous BOT will carry a signature in the user agent.

Note: You can visit https://www.iab.com/guidelines/iab-abc-international-spiders-bots-list/ to check out the paid list of existing BOTS.

The problem comes when either the publisher or the exchange or the DSP fails to filter this traffic, and the advertiser pays for a BOT generated traffic. This brings issues at the CPM-level buy.

I would still consider such BOTs as good ones because they are made for a specific purpose, but because the ad-tech stack does not or is unable to filter them out, the advertiser ends up paying for the BOT.

On the other hand, some BOTS are specifically made to generate traffic and clicks. As there is only ad-tech (exchange and DSP) and publishers who get paid by the advertising dollar, it is safe to say that such frauds can only happen if one of these players is involved.

BOT is essentially an app or a program that mimics human behavior. It does the following things:

1. Load the site or the app onto the browser/device.
2. Fire relevant triggers at UI or http level.
3. Repeat the process to generate scale.

As a malicious BOT can fake IP, UA profile, location, and so on, it can take advanced AI/ML-based solutions to figure out such patterns and block them.

A lot of bidders filter out fraud in their respective outlier systems. Outlier analysis covers many more cases beyond BOTS.

A good outlier identification system beyond BOTS can also figure out the media and audience that corresponds to traffic bounces, traffic generated by hackers, broken links, and so on.

Conclusion

Programmatic in-housing is a great option for an advertiser to create a Google and agency alternate system to create a capability for data drive media buy.

There are many aspects of data, media, and AI that are involved in establishing and operationalizing an in-housed programmatic system, and one must carefully examine all aspects of design, business goal, infrastructure, supply, data, and AI.

An understanding of measurement KPI, BOTS, attribution systems, and so on becomes very critical because they help in driving efficiencies at various levels. The following chapter focuses on the data privacy of users and the upcoming user data privacy regulations.

Questions

1. What is the checklist to in-house a bidder?

2. What role does data play in media buying?

Solutions

1. In-housing of a bidder can have many motivations. Nevertheless, a generic checklist can always help in getting the basics rights. It is as follows:

   a. Identify the data silos and ID mechanics.

   b. Put up a data strategy to manage in, out, and syncs of the data.

   c. Fix on the AI/ML that would be needed for the KPIs attainment.

   d. Figure out the supply sources.

   e. Fix and deploy bidder's data flows, callbacks, and bidding strategy.

   Start small and grow fast.

2. A statistically audience-based media buy strategy can achieve 30%+ better ROI. In some cases like re-targeting, audience-based targeting is a must. Audience give a lot of breadth and depth in the CDP in terms of a feature matrix. This makes audience play an important part of ad-tech.

CHAPTER 6
Data Privacy by Design

Introduction

The amount of data that is being generated by the internet today is unprecedented. In this new era of the internet and fast technologies, user data is getting misused and abused more and more frequently. Due to the misuse of such data, the privacy of each citizen of any country is at risk. It was high time that regulatory bodies came together to construct regulatory frameworks to stop such havoc from getting out of control. One of the first and foremost regulations that were formed was the **General Data Protection Regulation (GDPR)**. It was designed in 2016, and all relevant parties were given 2 years to implement the compliance. In May 2018, when the regulation came into effect in Europe and the UK region, the ad-tech industry, which is global, suddenly saw cracks in the design and simply could not cope up with the new scene. A lot of agencies pulled out of the region, and the global players simply isolated the audience-level targeting. This was a myopic view at its best. In an ideal world, the marketers and publishers should have had much better readiness for the upcoming change.

Right after the GDPR came into force, many other region-specific regulations were established, and these regulations were updated timely. This introduction of piecemeal regulation on the advertising industry has induced a lot of havoc. Despite rigorous measures, publishers and advertisers do not feel confident about the implications of the compliance.

Structure

- The data privacy landscape
- GDPR – the reference regulation
- The other regulations in play
- What does user privacy mean for the programmatic?
- Contextual versus audience targeting
- Privacy by design
- Incident management
- Consent traversal
- Data audit management
- Consent lifecycle

Objective

The objective of this chapter is to help understand the various aspects of data privacy and its navigation schematics. This may require prior knowledge of datasets being used in programmatic and also about the role played by marketers, publishers, and other ecosystem players.

The data privacy landscape

The talks of digital privacy in the face of data explosion have been on the table for over 2 decades now. This usually covers IT acts, financial data compliances, government data compliances, and so on. From an ad-tech perspective, where data is used at a large scale, having to comply with any meaningful regulation is only a few years old phenomena. This makes a lot of "Firsts" in implementing a compliance framework for any global operations.

Ad-tech from a technological perspective has always been a global play, and from a business perspective, it is always very local. The data regulations pan out at the state, country, or regions, which need to be implemented at the platform/technological level, and this creates unique challenges in understanding and implementing regulations.

A good example is, when the GDPR came into force, many non-EU/UK publishers and advertisers stopped using EU/UK data. This was not because the publishers or advertisers could not handle the technical aspects, but due to the uncertainty and risks associated with it.

Over a while, regulatory bodies in the USA, Canada, and so on had come up with similar regulations to protect their respective citizens. It will not be a far-fetched notion that most, if not all, of these regulations, are inspired by the GDPR.

The second issue and probably the more troubling aspect is the implementation of privacy aspects at the browser and OS level for apps that are being placed by Apple and Google. This would limit the ad-tech ecosystem to serve ads on third-party data.

Data privacy has been an afterthought, and needless to say, it is a huge change at the ecosystem level. No ecosystem player or platform can escape this change. Hence, it is needless to say that sooner or later, an advertiser and publisher will need to come out of isolation, understand the nuts and bolts, and imbibe the spirit of data privacy.

GDPR – the reference regulation

GDPR is the first large-scale regulation for data management. In all probability, many of the countries, and consequently the businesses, will adopt some of the other version of GDPR.

The working of the GDPR has been summarized as follows:

- GDPR is a framework to enable user privacy while protecting user privacy at the user level.

- There are three actors in the GDPR system: controller, processor, and supervisor. The lead supervisor is appointed by the government.

- The user (natural person) has the following rights:
    - All the information that is being processed should be accessible to the user.
    - The user should be aware of the identity of the controller and the purpose for acquiring the data.
    - The user has the right to get his profile deleted.
    - The users need to be able to follow up on the request of the above.
    - The user can register a complaint in the court of law in his/her city/ region or the controller's city/region.

- The regulations are applicable until and unless the identity of the user is anonymous. This makes the process of pseudonymization a very important part of the ecosystem.

- It is alright to track and profile a user with cookies and another digital generated post with adequate consent.

- The consent has to be explained in simple English. Explicit gains and all the purposes to acquire, retain, and process the data need to be captured. This makes a risk assessment of the data being collected a mandatory task.

- The controller, by design, owns the data and hence becomes liable to protect the user rights. The authority/responsibility of the controller includes complete omission of data, data portability, and also taking decisions based on profiling. Communications are to be carried out as well from the controller to the user in case of a breach of data.

- The **Supervisory Authority (SA)**, by design, ensures that the regulation is adhered to by the controllers and processors.

- A data breach needs to be reported to the SA.

- The controller should acquire data attributes that will fulfil the purpose. He/she needs to keep a minimalistic perspective on data achievement.

- The controller needs to keep a track of the user data because he/she will be exposed to the user. After all, he/she is responsible to protect the user's rights.

- The processor, by design, processes the data by adding attributes and creating new attributes. This also includes attributes based on aggregation.

- Children will benefit from the extra protection for the data that is being used.

- The controllers and processors need to coordinate within themselves to implement the regulations. The flow of data should be S2S. Here goes the problem of a walled garden.

- The SA will monitor data breach notifications and intervene when necessary.

- In case a controller or processor needs to consult the SA for review, consultations are made to keep the safeguards oiled up.

- Controllers and processors need to deploy a data protection officer who will represent data processes and compliances.

- SAs need to engage with the court of law in case any legal remedy needs to be obtained.

- SA can impose administrative fines and other penalties. Controllers and/or processors can challenge the decision in the court of law if they feel biased.

- Big entities need to cover themselves from legal aspects at all times.

- The SA, controllers, and processors need to give mechanisms to conduct reviews and audits.

There are many business opportunities in the new ecosystem. A transparent and clear data guideline will enable us to acquire a scale that was never possible.

The other regulations in play

The audience play that includes compliance becomes fairly complex. The following figure gives a high-level view of compliance, CDP, and its relationship.

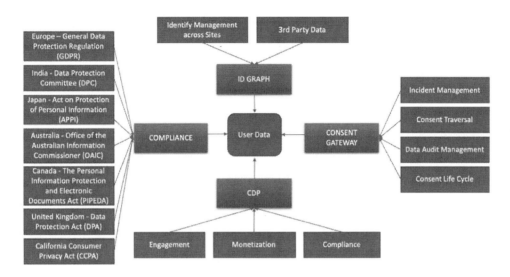

Figure 6.1: *User data paradigm*

The preceding figure tries to explain the ever-increasing complexities of the worldwide regulations that are on the ground or getting on the ground. Case in point, CCPA is a state-wide implementation of the data protection act in the California state of the USA. Florida, another state in the USA, has implemented Florida's Information Protection Act. This means that the USA itself may host multiple data protection regulations based on state boundaries.

Most of these regulations are still evolving. It will not be unfair to say that regulatory bodies and ad-tech ecosystems still have many gaps, and it has been a constant endeavor to close down those gaps. Even today, the ad-tech's implementation of user privacy is patchy at its best.

Meaning of privacy for the programmatic

User privacy is a broad term that means free from interference or intrusion. A user may or may not wish to share his or her confidential information. The user while browsing on the internet flushes out confidential information by filling out survey forms or login information while accessing any website or to provide feedback. A good publisher depends on the survival of the ad-revenue. This means exchanges, DMPs, CDPs, and DSPs along with tracking platforms, attribution systems, and so on are tracking a user via cookie, advertiser ID, or some other ID mechanics.

Most of this formal data is collected via consent. Needless to say, ad-tech has many black holes in the system, and any data breach is not surprising.

The compliance here makes it mandatory for all controllers to be able to put out a declaration before the information is being gathered from the user to make the data accessible for the generation of advertisements and related content while surfing the internet to increase engagement or traffic on the webpage. The consent must be clear, and the intent or purpose of what is being collected, how it is being collected, who all can access it for processing, and how long it will be stored must be disclosed. The controller hereby becomes liable for the protection of the user's data by default. The regulatory bodies have put forth compliance about the data being shared by the user where the CDP acts as a central repository to store all of the preferences and contact information of several users. It will also timestamp every stage of the data life cycle of the user. The function of a CDP is to lower the risk associated with the regulatory bodies, which could result in a hefty fine in case of a data breach. Engagement is the amount of traffic a website is receiving because of frequent visits by users on the website. The higher number of visitors means the engagement is more, hence increasing traffic on the page.

Contextual targeting versus audience targeting

Audience targeting means when the ad rendered for the user has considered the user profile. There are many ways to do that, but the bottom line is that the system will need to have a user ID in place, a profile that is built on that ID, and an ad-serving mechanics that uses this profile ID. Certain demographics help in separating consumers into segments based on this data. The demographics that can help determine are age, gender, average income, location, interests, and so on. Psychological demographics can also be helpful. One must focus on the type of consumers for a particular product or campaign. The critical assessment of the analytics of a website is very important in audience targeting. A variety of survey and feedback programs can help in the determination of the interests of the target audience before officially launching any product or service. Running personalized and creative ads is very useful in this context as well.

On the other hand, contextual targeting takes the media attributes into account and serves the advertisement accordingly. In this mechanics, no user profile is used. Contextual targeting works on a different algorithm. It scans specific keywords, the text of a website, and so on. After scanning, it accordingly returns advertisements based on those keywords. Advertising platforms will then analyze your content to figure out the core theme. Then, the content of your website is matched against the browsing history, location, related topics, and other factors.

From a user perspective, irrespective of handing out consent and sharing data, he/she will always see an ad. This makes me wonder that as a user it is probably better to give consent and see relevant ads than to not give consent and see irrelevant ads.

Privacy by design

In this spiral world of data, the data owners seek ways and means to monetize the data. Typically, the first-party data holder can also be referred to as the data owner. Other players who work with third-party data or use data in the up/down phenomena to stream data do so to effectively execute its tasks. The following figure explains about the three kinds of data seekers:

Figure 6.2: Supply path

Publishers and, to some extent, even the advertisers have direct access to the user and hence possess user data. Both of them typically would take consent from the user to use the data to various degrees. The consent would also entail the right to send this data upstream/download to SSPs, DSPs, and DMPs/CDPs for managing supply and demand. For business reasons, a publisher will have a far more number of users but a general taxonomy for the users. On the other hand, an advertiser would have a much lesser number of users but will have very in-depth taxonomies describing the user.

The following figure explains the components that are typically used to attain compliance. This can also constitute a consent management system. The three kinds of entities mentioned in preceding *Figure 6.2* would need to have a touchpoint with them:

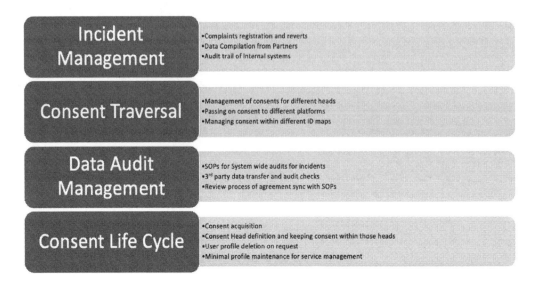

Figure 6.3: *Consent facets*

The consent management system is used by third-party apps and websites to authenticate the identity of a user and receive permission to access their information. For example, while making a payment on any of the online websites, the website does not have a payment gateway of its own. It is always redirected to a payment gateway hosted by a third party that sends the user an OTP to authenticate the user's identity. As soon as the user enters the digits, the controller gets access to make a successful payment, and the data technically may or may not be stored. But again, in the present times, data theft is a massive issue around the world, and hence, the regulations for these are of utmost importance.

Incident management

An incident is a typical data breach, a user requisition for the deletion, or a compliance-related event. A data owner should have processes to handle such incidents.

One of the primary premises is that precursor to the implementation of incident management the vulnerability in data transmission, stored data, and its flows need to be analyzed to templatize incidents.

The three components of a good incident management system are as follows:

- **Ticket system**: A ticket system is a templatized representation of the reported incident. The incident could be internal or external. A set of detailed ticket templates would constitute various data complaints, breaches, and risk scenarios. A detailed ticket mechanic only means that the data owner has taken enough measures to comply with the regulations.

- **Partner management**: There are many aspects to partner management. Some of the aspects that need to be covered are as follows:

  o **Liability**: The data liability needs to be distributed. This stems from the fact that liability is directly proportional to the access to data and the sensitive information that it may pertain to.

  o **Data management processes**: The ad-tech ecosystem works in a mesh model, and hence, the data also flows similarly. As a controller or data owner, the data management process should cover all the states of data between all internal and external business modules and/or partners.

  o **Data trails**: It is important to map all the processes related to data, including storage, use cases, and **Extract, Transform, and Load** (ETL) functions, at every stage.

An incident, in the data paradigm, is inevitable. A grounds up preparation is the only way to be perpetually ready. Where 90% of the incidents should be manageable via templatized response, 10% may require a more direct involvement.

The ticketing system helps to templatize incidents. A ticketing system will need to be integrated with all the customer interfaces. It typically helps communicate with the end customer on all notices and responses.

A few sample incidents are as follows:

- A user may ask the publisher or data controller to give his/her profile.

- A user may seek to delete his/her profile.

- A user may seek to modify his/her profile.

- A user may seek not to be tracked.

- A data breach may have occurred, and the data owner would need to inform the user.

Note: A user interacts with the publisher or advertiser via an incident management system.

Consent traversal

Consent traversal means two things in ad-serving:

1. A user profile is picked to show the ad when the user has agreed to it.

2. A user profile is not picked to show the ad.

From a publisher to DSP, there are many stakeholders in the supply chain. This means that if the user has opted for option 2, then the exchange and/or DSP cannot use the user profile.

Consent traversal also constitutes that if the user has asked the consent system to "Not Track" him/her, then the publishers, exchanges, ad-networks, and DSPs cannot even continue to track the user.

> **Note: This means that a publisher needs to ensure that the third-party cookies, typically used by the exchange and DSPs, need to be included in the consent framework.**

As the DSPs and exchanges use their IDs to track/profile a user, the publisher may end up having multiple such exchanges. An effective consent traversal may require the publisher to connect with all of them to execute any incident ticket.

For example, once a user asks the publisher to delete the profile, a publisher may need to go to all the exchanges and DSPs and ensure that this profile delete instruction has been executed. Post this, the user also needs to be updated about the incident response.

Data audit management

A data audit management can be defined as a means by which any organization can access or identify data in a framework. The consent life cycle is data transmission between systems that ensures the current consent preferences of the user have been updated. An ID graph basically will hold all the data of several users and pick out correlatives to target a particular audience sector.

The CDP helps brands to meet compliance quickly and efficiently. All of the preceding have specific functions or attributes that work in a framework to ensure that data breach does not occur and defines the relationship between CDP and compliance, which has been laid down by the regulatory.

> **Note: An ID graph helps connect multiple IDs for the same user.**

Consent life cycle

In both scenarios of device ID (IDFA/GAID) and cookie, the publisher has to ask the user for consent. As per the compliance guidelines, the publisher has to explain why such tracking is necessary. Compliance also states that minimal data has to be collected for any given task.

There are two parts to consent as follows:

- A user has to accept the cookie, drop or choose otherwise.
- Publishers categorize the cookies, and the user is given the choice between the cookie groups, as a general practice. Every group is explained in easy and understandable language.

Acquisition of consent is the first step in the consent life cycle.

Using the consent to approve the usage of the user profile is the second step. IAB standards suggest the usage of the consent string. Essentially, the consent acquired is to be sent to the DSPs via exchanges so that they can use the consent for user targeting.

The last step of the consent life cycle is the deletion of the consent. A user typically goes to the publisher and requests for profile delete. At this point, the publisher needs to access all the internal modules, CRMs, partners, and so on so that the sync and profiles are deleted.

Conclusion

It is safe to say that user privacy is an integral part of the ad-tech ecosystem. A worldwide user privacy paradigm is currently fragmented and gradually building up. A publisher or a marketer who deals with a worldwide audience has to rather deal with many contradictory regulatory requirements.

In addition, browser companies such as Safari (Apple), Firefox, Chrome, and so on are deprecating third-party cookie support.

Publishers and marketers who work with audience-based targeting are finding the privacy framework tedious and confusing at best. A holistic "Privacy by Design" has to be understood and probably is the only way to go.

A holistic approach to the consent management system that is implemented by design would solve a lot of regulatory problems and help the publisher and marketer to solve today's problems and become future-ready.

Chapter 7 helps to formulate the strategies for in-housing. In essence, it tries to build a high-level view of where the different pieces that are covered in this book will fit in an overall in-housing strategy.

Questions

1. What is a consent framework?
2. What are the challenges one might face while implementing user privacy?

Solutions

1. User consent is the permission to use the user data for specific purposes. A consent framework manages three things:

    a. Acquisition of the consent

    b. Propagate the consent to the relevant systems and comply with the regulations of track, modify, and deletion of the consent

    c. Activate compliance in the relevant data pipe/s as and when the need arises

2. There are many challenges in managing user privacy. The top three of them are as follows:

    a. Consolidation of data at the source

    b. Mapping the data pipes within the organization and partners

    c. Creating a consolidated legal framework for all data blocks within the organization and with partners

CHAPTER 7
In-Housing – The Way Forward

Introduction

For a key stakeholder who is looking into the in-housing of programmatic, it takes enormous insight, skills, and commitment to take this journey. This chapter helps in providing some methods to access the current status and readiness to move forward. This chapter covers not only the ways and means to take key decisions but also ensures that all the critical factors are covered.

This chapter ties all the previous topics together. As programmatic in-housing needs an understanding of the CDP, bidder, and/or exchange, one needs to have some understanding of these systems to understand this chapter better. From another point of view, one can read this chapter and bounce back and forth to connect all the dots in one go.

Advertisers and publishers take different paths to manage their business goals. In-housing provides them with various options and so on. However, key decisions remain very similar.

Structure

- Key goals
- Self-assessment

- Understanding the supply chain
- In-housing – Goal 1 - manage supply chain effectively:
  - o Architecture
  - o Advertiser
  - o Data in-housed and looking for the next step
  - o Publisher
- Key factors for consideration:
  - o Build versus buy
  - o Talent
  - o Duopoly
  - o Transparency
  - o Privacy
  - o Auction
  - o Relationships
  - o Short/long-term strategy

Objective

The reader needs to understand the data collection, data strategy, AI options, and buy/sell systems before one can get into formulating any plan. In-housing by definition is custom deployment. This means that every tool and concept has to be retrofitted within the over strategy and tech stack of the advertiser or publisher.

Key goals

The baseline logic is to encompass all media buy and sell functions. Primarily, there are things related to user and media, which are as follows:

- Advertisers:
  - o Brand:
    - ▪ Brand reach and recall
    - ▪ Brand to product connect
  - o User engagement:
    - ▪ Prospecting
    - ▪ Cross/upselling

- Publishers:
  - Monetization:
    - Optimizing media's price ask
    - Optimizing audience's price ask
  - Engagement:
    - Generation of traffic
    - Cross/upselling

A good source of information for an advertiser's in-housing is available with IAB. IAB stands for Interactive Advertising Bureau. It does a lot of work for bringing the specifications and roadmap for the media trading tools.

Surprisingly, there are no benchmarks and/or roadmaps that are published by the IAB for the publishers.

Anyways, some of the key goals in-housing are as follows:

1. Advertiser:
   a. ROI – buy efficiency
   b. Audience targeting and better match rates
   c. Campaign effectiveness
   d. Optimization
   e. Customer data management
   f. Media planning
   g. Audience reach and targeting
   h. Manage data compliance risks

2. Publisher:
   a. ROI – sell efficiency
   b. Audience extension
   c. Manage data compliance risk
   d. Customer data management

Self-assessment

In-housing for advertisers and publishers is always a very big decision. In all fairness, this usually consists of many steps. A typical in-housing journey has been described in the following figure:

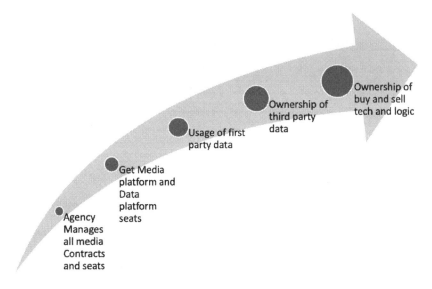

Figure 7.1: Roadmap to programmatic in-housing

The preceding figure shows the key milestones for in-housing. Some of the characteristics of these milestones are explained as follows:

Step 1: Agency manages all media contracts and seats

This is a well-known format by advertisers. In some cases, publishers may also have some connections with the agencies. However, in most cases, a publisher would opt for a DFP, Index, PubMatic, ION seat, and so on. Hence, in most of the publisher's cases, this step is usually skipped.

The impact of the preceding is as follows:

1. Capable to run programmatic campaigns
2. Basic targeting and campaign operation

Step 2: Get media platform and data platform seats

Firstly, an agency plays a very important role in media activation (running of campaigns) and delivers a lot of value in terms of innovative creativity. A good way for an advertiser and publisher is to get the media and data seats and let them manage the accounts. This way, the trading desk is still maintained by the agency.

The impact of the preceding is as follows:

1. Agency commission and platform fees clarity

2. Better reports

3. Campaign operational efficiencies

Step 3: Usage of first-party data

Usage of first-party data in buying or selling is a big step. Currently, there is only one use case of re-targeting that uses the first-party data. There could be many more cases; some of them are as follows:

1. **Publishers:**

    a. Metadata enrichment

    b. First-party data-based ad-serving

2. **Advertiser:**

    a. First-party data-based targeting

    b. First-party data-based lookalikes for prospecting

    c. First-party data-based cross-selling and upselling

    d. Layering second-party data to extend the data reach

The impact of the preceding is as follows:

1. High-impact audience-based targeting

2. Manage frauds to an extent

Step 4: Ownership of third-party data

There are ~100x data beyond impressions, clicks, and conversion data. Unless there is the technology that can help build and use this data in the universe, until then, this data stays unusable. Yes, I am talking about RTB streams.

The impact of the preceding is as follows:

1. Attaining scale

2. Effective outlier identification

Step 5: Ownership of buy and sell tech and logic

In today's time, every buy and sell happens via AI. The statement suggests that the publisher and advertiser own data, tech, and AI layers to manage buys and sells.

The impact of the preceding is as follows:

1. Optimize supply chain

2. Sustainable buy and sell metrics

Understanding the supply chain

Programmatic has one of the most complex supply chains. Many studies have been done by various bodies. The essences of these are as follows:

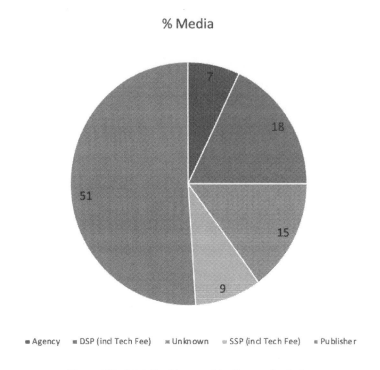

Figure 7.2: *Ad-dollar % payout in the supply chain*

The advertising money spills over in the following way:

Advertiser | Agency | DSP | SSP | Publisher

One of the biggest issues with this figure is the unknown 15% that simply lands in the unknown pockets.

The study consisted of the following stakeholders:

1. 8 agency

2. 5 DSP

3. 5 SSP

4. 12 publishers

PWC found 290 unique supply chains. If we consider 5 DSP, 5 SSP, and 12 publishers, then the maximum supply chain possible is 5 × 5 × 12 = 300. Because all the 12 publishers would have had header bidding systems in place and the supply would reach all DSP.

> **Note: I have referred to a supply chain audit summary study done by ISBA and PWC for the UK market that was released in the mid of 2020.**

Header bidding, by design, was created to compete with DFP. Prebid.org was primarily driven by companies that wanted to compete with DFP and were not getting a foothold.

Header bidding systems can conduct an auction at their end and that data is hidden from Google. However, the primary auction was still conducted by DFP. There are a lot of controversies that Google does not play fair when dealing with header bidding mechanics.

> **Note: DFP and Adx are ad-server and exchange of the Google stack. For a long time, it was unclear about what auction does DFP use to handle header bidding-based demand.**

The advent of exchange bidding by Google was to overshadow header bidding systems. For obvious reasons, it is in Google's interest to keep it this way and use the vantage point to drive profits.

In-housing – Goal 1 - manage supply chain effectively

Let us talk about the hardest part first. For both advertisers and publishers, managing the supply chain for sustainable ROI is very important.

In today's world, the programmatic supply chain looks such as described in the following figure:

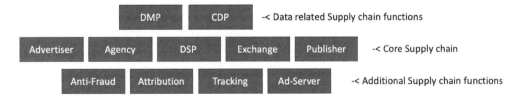

Figure 7.3: High-level supply chain for biddable media

1. The core supply chain contains minimal building blocks.

2. The additional supply chain functions are loosely coupled with the core block.

3. The data-related supply chain functions work in parallel and integrate at all the levels in the core supply chain.

As a ground rule – an advertiser should look at SSP and publisher as a supply source, and the publisher needs to look at DSP and SSP as a demand source. This process allows control of the middle hops.

Note: It is a known fact that players who manage the end-to-end supply chain and hold the power to manipulate the prices at both the ends, that is, advertiser continuously pays more and more and the publisher continuously gets lesser and lesser. The only way to introduce a new supply part is to eliminate one or more hop.

This looks very obvious, but today, very few advertisers or publishers have any sense of supply paths and their sources. Most of them do not have any view beyond Google.

A pure in-housing ecosystem would look such as described in the following figure:

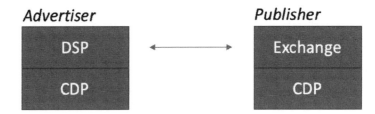

Figure 7.4: In-housed scenario for a brand

The functions of attribution, tracking, and so on are incorporated into CDP. The following figure has the simplest format that depicts the working of an in-housing ecosystem. In the purest in-housing format, this can be achieved as follows:

1. **For advertisers**:
    - ○ Host a bidder.
    - ○ Host a CDP with relevant AI packages.
    - ○ Connect data pipes of CRM and other data partners.
    - ○ Find out the relevant and long-tail publishers and get connected to direct exchanges.
    - ○ Set up a trading desk and a creative team.
    - ○ Start buying media.

2. **For publisher**:
    - ○ Host a CDP.

- o Host a private exchange that can source demand from ad-tags and RTB.

- o Connect data pipes to metadata enrichment.

- o Find out relevant and long-tail demand partners.

- o Set up an operations team for direct demand (considering one has direct demand).

- o Start selling media.

Few things that will further be required to fire up the system and be essential to the working are as follows:

1. A consent management system that ensures the ad is served with compliance.

2. In the case of advertisers, media buying requires a large set of media exposure. One may require integrating with traditional programmatic exchanges to get access to a large % of the market.

3. In the case of publishers, media selling requires immediate access to demand, as a direct exchange one can look at other SSPs and DSPs for demand.

The impact of the preceding is as follows:

From DSP to SPP and everyone in between, the supply chain charges upward of 50% of ad-dollar. For all theoretical purposes, if an advertiser buys media from a publisher on a one-to-one basis, then this advertiser can buy the same media at half the cost.

Hence, in a real-life environment, on account of supply chain optimizations:

1. Advertisers can expect 20–30% better ROI

2. Publishers can expect 15–25% better ROI

Essentially, 51% gets distributed between the advertiser and the publisher.

Architecture

It is important to understand that a good architecture gives a business many advantages such as:

1. Better ROI

2. Faster operational turnarounds

3. Future-proofing of business

Advertiser

In the programmatic ecosystem, an advertiser is the one who pays the bills of all the parties involved. This makes him/her one of the most important stakeholders. There are many things that an advertiser should keep in mind. Some of them are as follows:

1. Every answer will be provided by data. Ensure all media buy decisions are backed by data.

2. Media is a commodity, but right media is always a challenge.

3. Ensure that the media plan encompasses various digital channels, and attribution can tie them up together.

4. The creative aspect of media buy should be addressed adequately.

Two primary scenarios arise when looking at in-house. They are as follows:

Greenfield

A very rare phenomenon takes place because an advertiser will not want to in-house unless they are having some buy functions already in place.

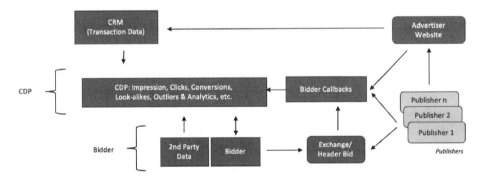

Figure 7.5: High-level view of in-housed DSP for a brand

This is the least effort deployment. Needless to say that it will take the least amount of time.

> **Note: It always takes an experienced and a well-articulated team to handle an in-housing project. A green field project can only be executed by new blood that is experienced and can manage expectations at the management level.**

As explained in the preceding figure, an advertiser hosts the following:

1. CDP helps the bidder with data and relevant algorithms.

2. The bidder is the actual media buy tool.

Bidders get supply from the exchange and the relevant RTB level callbacks. CDP is connected to CRM and is using CRM data in a second-party data format.

Brownfield

Let us assume that the marketer has a DSP seat, and they use the seat for media and data buy. An advanced buyer may also be using first-party data via CRM and so on. It is safe to say that every in-housing project brings unique data onto the table, and that brings in unique challenges.

Beyond the greenfield projects, *Figure 7.6* shows the following:

1. A common CDP feeds data into DBM/equivalent. This ensures that the two bidders can work in parallel at the audience level.

2. As impression callbacks are RTB protocol-governed, it will happen at two places that need to be managed at the operational level.

Note: This is the most common scenario with in-housing. DBM and DV360 are the same platform, but different versions.

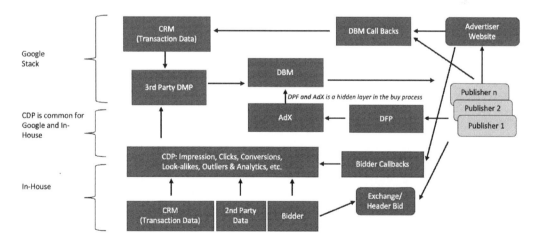

Figure 7.6: *High-level view of in-housed DSP for a brand*

One of the primary requirements of the in-housing of the bidder can be to work in tandem with DV360, TTD, or any other DSP in parallel. It becomes imperative that a strategy be derived where two bidders can work together.

This is Stage 1, as described in self-assessment *Figure 7.1.*

Data in-housed and looking for the next step

Usually, the first step of in-housing begins with the in-housing of data. Once that is done, one would look at additional buy functions.

A large advertiser usually has a CRM system that stores customer history, profile, complaints, and so on. This CRM data can be overlaid on top of bid-stream data via CDP. These CRM segments can further be used for re-targeting. Further, they can be used as reference segments for lookalikes for prospecting. With the right strategy, CRM segments can play a vital role in media buy to drive brand recall and transactions.

Publisher

In the programmatic ecosystem, the publisher has one of the most critical roles of generating quality supply and catering to the content needs of the audience. Essentially, there are three things that a publisher should look at:

1. **Fair auction mechanics**: This ensures that all demand sources are given equal opportunity.

2. **Multiple demand sources**: This means that the demand is acquired from multiple sources.

3. **Optimal floor price**: This is a critical piece in all media sell.

A relatively simple scenario for a publisher is described in the following figure:

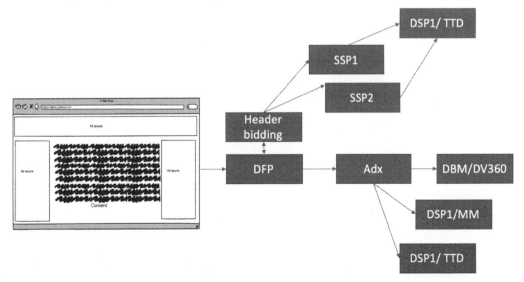

Figure 7.7: High-level view of in-housed DSP for a publisher

In the preceding figure, a publisher is getting parallel demand from header bidding systems. The rest of the stack remains in the following sequence:

The publisher configures ad-units on DFP/ad-server or any other ad-server.

The ad-server gives our ad-request to Adx (the first exchange/Google's exchange) or any other exchange.

Adx further gives the request to other SSPs and DSPs.

This scenario caters to the second point of having multiple demand sources.

An ideal scenario that caters to multiple demand partners, fair auction systems, and optimized floor price is depicted in the following figure:

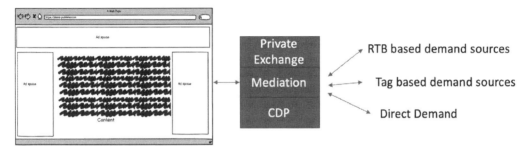

Figure 7.8: High-level view of in-housed DSP for a publisher

Key factors for consideration

There are many articles and IAB reports that talk about the challenges of in-housing. A lot of reports conclude that in-housing is too tough due to the challenges it poses. I have just one argument, that is, if in-housing can fetch you even 20% better ROI while reducing/eliminating the data compliance risk and gives better control on the buy/sell process, then moving forward with in-housing seemingly has enough motivation.

The following text focuses on the possible ways to solve the problem rather than explaining the problem in detail, which I think everyone knows to various degrees. Having said all that, some factors create various degrees of impact, and those cannot be ignored.

Build versus buy

For a successful in-housing project, one requires a skilled team. The functions are as follows:

1. Core modules (backend systems)

2. UI/ UX

3. Infrastructure designing

4. AI/ML

5. Supply/demand/data relationship management

6. Business-driven architecture

7. Team/CXO management

Skill will come from experience and knowledge. In-housing takes 1 year to set a baseline and another 2 years to scale. It requires skilled and seasoned people to exert this kind of energy and focus.

The real question is – where do you find a team with enough skills and be smart enough to pull off this kind of a project? Assuming you have an internal team that feels confident to carry the work; I would say this is a best-case scenario. More often than not, you will end up searching for people outside of your company.

One common mistake that people make is to underestimate the effort, and they begin to start the project internally/externally without allocating adequate resources. This is a key recipe for disaster.

Talent

There is no escaping from getting a skilled team. Irrespective of the decision of putting an internal and external team, one will also need to be vigilant of the ever-changing dynamics of the business requirements and its supporting tech and operational skills.

A cross-functional ad-tech team will comprise of the following:

Assuming one already owns a DSP/SSP seat, then they will only require:

1. Operations personal

2. Business P&L

In-housing entails a large set of functions ranging from engineering, AI, operations, and business development; they are as follows:

1. **Engineering:**
   o Backend
   o Frontend

2. **AI/ML:**
   o Operations for day-to-day optimization
   o New models

3. **Operations:**
   o Acquiring and tuning media
   o Acquiring and tuning data
   o Acquiring and tuning demand

4. **Business development:**
   o Platform-to-platform partnerships
   o Managing day-to-day relationships

5. **Architect:**
   o Owner of the roadmap
   o Ensures operational efficiency

I often hear that getting talent is challenging. However, in most cases, understanding talent is the real problem. With enough time and money, talent can be either created or acquired.

Duopoly

Duopoly is a term generally used for the combination consisting of Facebook and Google and the fact that they take 50–70% of the marketer's budget.

Where Facebook is a publisher and Google is a search and programmatic platform (among other things), the term duopoly covers a wide range of services/functions.

By design, in-housing is an alternative to the Google programmatic ecosystem. I am specifically not calling this a Google platform or solution because they are a whole host of services, tools, and platforms with various entry and exit points for all players, that is, marketers, agency, SSP, and publisher.

If an advertiser and publisher can think pragmatically about in-housing, then Facebook and Google can be treated as digital marketing channels while using other media channels.

Transparency

The programmatic supply chain has always eluded people. It was simpler to gauge in the early days, but today, it is simply impossible to get an end-to-end view.

In my view, transparency has two aspects, which are as follows:

1. The marketer could know what the publisher gets.
2. The seller should know what the marketer has paid.

Easier said than done, to achieve something like this, all media commissions and hops and third service need to be known.

As the in-housing undertaking, where transparency can be achieved, this needs to be done to attain ROI.

Privacy

One needs to be aware of the regulatory paradigm when dealing with data. Every serious publisher and marketer needs to use a user consent management system that is connected to CDP and forwardly integrated with buy/sell infrastructure.

Privacy by design needs to happen for any long-term in-housing plan.

Auction

In a world of header bidding, exchange bidding, and unknown media margins, understanding of auctions and their business impacts is essential to quantify the quality of the supply chain.

Every SSP hop will have some auction taking place. More hops mean more auctions. More hops mean the actual bid that you have bid did not make till the SSP for conducting the auction.

The quality media is always limited and usually hard to find in the ever-complex supply chain.

Do not be surprised if the same publisher works for you in a different supply chain.

Relationships

A big part of in-housing is partnership management. It is a straightforward requirement – SSPs need DSPs, and DSPs need SSPs.

So, a marketer has to look out for the right media sources by talking directly to the publisher or the aggregators and vice-versa. This is typically a platform-to-platform deal and has its fair share of operational challenges.

Platforms typically come with infrastructure costs that are fixed in nature. After all, the dynamic optimization and so on will end up having a minimal cost. This means that to have a positive ROI, this cost needs to be accommodated in the total equation. Hence, this can only be achieved by running the system with basic minimal business.

As the major part of the ad-tech industry works on revenue share, all the platforms ask for minimal business. This becomes a challenge for the in-house systems that are still trying to settle down in the first year.

A strong relationship is required to set up demand/supply pipes in the beginning to avoid the cold start problem. This is usually done by doing a 2–3-year projection and stating that a percentage of current business would be shifted to the in-house system.

Short/long-term strategy

It takes time, team, and business goals to execute any good in-housing project. The second in line are supply, demand, and technology (engineering and AI).

It takes over a few iterations to set up a good buy and sell system.

The most common problems in all the failed in-housing projects that I have seen are as follows:

1. No dedicated resources
2. No product/service roadmap
3. Shortage of skill
4. Not enough testing time
5. Not enough testing budget
6. No top-level buy-in
7. Too soon to give up

Try to escape them!!!

Conclusion

An alternative to the Google ecosystem is the tall claim that in-housing does. Ad-tech is a multi-billion-dollar business, and the top 5 players all make a billion-dollar revenue.

In print advertising, the middlemen take about 15% of the media commission. In programmatic, the commission ranges from 35 to 80%. If you ask any economist, this kind of commission model is simply unsustainable for the industry.

In-housing helps in attaining control, transparency, and better ROI for both marketers and publishers.

Questions

1. As a publisher, how do you adopt in-housing?
2. As an advertiser, how do you adopt in-housing?

Solution

1. As a publisher who wants advertising as a revenue line needs to look at the monetization stack. Essentially, a publisher needs to have a view on the demand sources, a mediation stack that can do justice with the demand sources, and data that will help it fetch better eCPM. A tech and data framework needs to be finalized that delivers the mediation template and data.

2. As an advertiser, one needs to understand the marketing goals and translate them into media and data requirements. These media and data requirements may constantly change. Hence, a generic supply path needs to be considered to accommodate a variety of requirement changes. Post that, a data strategy and a bidding strategy needs to be contemplated. All these things put together will help in arriving at a solution and/or service.

Annexure 1

Bid Request Specifica-tion 3.1 Object Model	Object	Section	Description	Spec 2.3	Spec 2.4	Spec 2.5
	Bid Request	3.2.1	Top-level object.	YES	YES	YES
	Source	3.2.2	Request source details on post-auction decisioning (e.g., header bidding).	No	No	YES
	Regs	3.2.3	Regulatory conditions in effect for all impressions in this bid request.	YES	YES	YES
	Imp	3.2.4	Container for the description of a specific impression; at least 1 per request.	YES	YES	YES
	Metric	3.2.5	A quantifiable often historical data point about an impression.	No	No	YES

Banner	3.2.6	Details for a banner impression (including in-banner video) or video companion ad.	YES	YES	YES
Video	3.2.7	Details for a video impression.	YES	YES	YES
Audio	3.2.8	Container for an audio impression.	No	YES	YES
Native	3.2.9	Container for a native impression conforming to the Dynamic Native Ads API.	YES	YES	YES
Format	3.2.10	An allowed size of a banner.	No	YES	YES
Pmp	3.2.11	Collection of Private Marketplace (PMP) deals applicable to this impression.	YES	YES	YES
Deal	3.2.12	Deal terms pertaining to this impression between a seller and buyer.	YES	YES	YES
Site	3.2.13	Details of the website calling for the impression.	YES	YES	YES
App	3.2.14	Details of the application calling for the impression.	YES	YES	YES
Publisher	3.2.15	Entity that controls the content of and distributes the site or app.	YES	YES	YES
Content	3.2.16	Details about the published content itself, within which the ad will be shown.	YES	YES	YES
Producer	3.2.17	Producer of the content; not necessarily the publisher (e.g., syndication).	YES	YES	YES
Device	3.2.18	Details of the device on which the content and impressions are displayed.	YES	YES	YES
Geo	3.2.19	Location of the device or user's home base depending on the parent object.	YES	YES	YES
User	3.2.20	Human user of the device; audience for advertising.	YES	YES	YES
Data	3.2.21	Collection of additional user targeting data from a specific data source.	YES	YES	YES

| Segment | 3.2.22 | Specific data point about a user from a specific data source. | YES | YES | YES |

3.2.1 Object: Bid Request	Attribute	Type	Description			
	id	string; re-quired	Unique ID of the bid request, provided by the exchange.	YES	YES	YES
	imp	object array; re-quired	Array of Imp objects (Section 3.2.4) representing the impressions offered. At least 1 Imp object is required.	YES	YES	YES
	site	object; recom-mend-ed	Details via a Site object (Section 3.2.13) about the publisher's website. Only applicable and recommended for websites.	YES	YES	YES
	app	object; recom-mend-ed	Details via an App object (Section 3.2.14) about the publisher's app (i.e., non-browser applications). Only applicable and recommended for apps.	YES	YES	YES
	device	object; recom-mend-ed	Details via a Device object (Section 3.2.18) about the user's device to which the impression will be delivered.	YES	YES	YES
	user	object; recom-mend-ed	Details via a User object (Section 3.2.20) about the human user of the device; the advertising audience.	YES	YES	YES
	test	integer; default 0	Indicator of test mode in which auctions are not billable, where 0 = live mode, 1 = test mode.	YES	YES	YES
	at	integer; default 2	Auction type, where 1 = first price, 2 = second price plus. Exchange-specific auction types can be defined using values greater than 500.	YES	YES	YES

tmax	integer	Maximum time in milliseconds the exchange allows for bids to be received, including Internet latency to avoid timeout. This value supersedes any a priori guidance from the exchange.	YES	YES	YES
wseat	string array	White list of buyer seats (e.g., advertisers, agencies) allowed to bid on this impression. IDs of seats and knowledge of the buyer's customers to which they refer must be coordinated between bidders and the exchange a priori. At most, only one of wseat and bseat should be used in the same request. Omission of both implies no seat restrictions.	YES	YES	YES
bseat	string array	Block list of buyer seats (e.g., advertisers, agencies) restricted from bidding on this impression. IDs of seats and knowledge of the buyer's customers to which they refer must be coordinated between bidders and the exchange a priori. At most, only one of wseat and bseat should be used in the same request. Omission of both implies no seat restrictions.	No	No	YES
allimps	integer; default 0	Flag to indicate if the exchange can verify that the impressions offered represent all of the impressions available in context (e.g., all on the webpage, all video spots such as pre/mid/post-roll) to support road-blocking. 0 = no or unknown, 1 = yes, the impressions offered represent all that are available.	YES	YES	YES

	cur	string	Array of allowed currencies for bids on this bid request using ISO-4217 alpha codes. Recommended only if the exchange accepts multiple currencies.	YES	YES	YES
	wlang	string array	White list of languages for creatives using ISO-639-1-alpha-2. Omission implies no specific restrictions, but buyers would be advised to consider language attribute in the Device and/or Content objects if available.	No	No	YES
	bcat	string array	Blocked advertiser categories using the IAB content categories. Refer to List 5.1.	YES	YES	YES
	badv	string array	Block list of advertisers by their domains (e.g., "ford.com").	YES	YES	YES
	bapp	string array	Block list of applications by their platform-specific exchange-independent application identifiers. On Android, these should be bundle or package names (e.g., com.foo.mygame). On iOS, these are numeric IDs.	No	YES	YES
	source	object	A Source object (Section 3.2.2) that provides data about the inventory source and which entity makes the final decision.	No	No	YES
	regs	object	A Regs object (Section 3.2.3) that specifies any industry, legal, or governmental regulations in force for this request.	YES	YES	YES
	ext	object	Placeholder for exchange-specific extensions to OpenRTB.	YES	YES	YES

3.2.2 Object: Source	Attribute	Type	Description			
	fd	Integer; recom-mend-ed	Entity responsible for the final impression sale decision, where 0 = exchange, 1 = upstream source.	No	No	YES
	tid	string; recom-mend-ed	Transaction ID that must be common across all participants in this bid request (e.g., potentially multiple exchanges).	No	No	YES
	pchain	string; recom-mend-ed	Payment ID chain string containing embedded syntax described in the TAG Payment ID Protocol v1.0.	No	No	YES
	ext	object	Placeholder for exchange-specific extensions to OpenRTB.	No	No	YES

3.2.3 Object: Regs	Attribute	Type	Description			
	coppa	integer	Flag indicating if this request is subject to the COPPA regulations established by the USA FTC, where 0 = no, 1 = yes. Refer to Section 7.5 for more information.	YES	YES	YES
	ext	object	Placeholder for exchange-specific extensions to OpenRTB.	YES	YES	YES

3.2.4 Object: Imp	Attribute	Type	Description			
	id	string; re-quired	A unique identifier for this impression within the context of the bid request (typically, starts with 1 and increments.	YES	YES	YES

metric	object array	An array of the Metric object (Section 3.2.5).	No	No	YES
banner	object	A Banner object (Section 3.2.6); required if this impression is offered as a banner ad opportunity.	YES	YES	YES
video	object	A Video object (Section 3.2.7); required if this impression is offered as a video ad opportunity.	YES	YES	YES
audio	object	An Audio object (Section 3.2.8); required if this impression is offered as an audio ad opportunity.	No	YES	YES
native	object	A Native object (Section 3.2.9); required if this impression is offered as a native ad opportunity.	YES	YES	YES
pmp	object	A Pmp object (Section 3.2.11) containing any private marketplace deals in effect for this impression.	YES	YES	YES
display-manager	string	Name of ad mediation partner, SDK technology, or player responsible for rendering an ad (typically, video or mobile). Used by some ad servers to customize ad code by partner. Recommended for video and/or apps.	YES	YES	YES
display-managerver	string	Version of ad mediation partner, SDK technology, or player responsible for rendering ad (typically, video or mobile). Used by some ad servers to customize ad code by partner. Recommended for video and/or apps.	YES	YES	YES
instl	integer; default 0	1 = the ad is interstitial or full screen, 0 = not interstitial.	YES	YES	YES

tagid	string	Identifier for specific ad placement or ad tag that was used to initiate the auction. This can be useful for debugging of any issues, or for optimization by the buyer.	YES	YES	YES
bidfloor	float; default 0	Minimum bid for this impression expressed in CPM.	YES	YES	YES
bidfloorcur	string; default "USD"	Currency specified using ISO-4217 alpha codes. This may be different from bid currency returned by the bidder if this is allowed by the exchange.	YES	YES	YES
clickbrows-er	integer	Indicates the type of browser opened upon clicking the creative in an app, where 0 = embedded, 1 = native. Note that the Safari View Controller in iOS 9.x devices is considered a native browser for purposes of this attribute.	No	YES	YES
secure	integer	Flag to indicate if the impression requires secure HTTPS URL creative assets and markup, where 0 = non-secure, 1 = secure. If omitted, the secure state is unknown, but non-secure HTTP support can be assumed.	YES	YES	YES
iframe-buster	string array	Array of exchange-specific names of supported iframe busters.	YES	YES	YES
exp	integer	Advisory as to the number of seconds that may elapse between the auction and the actual impression.	No	YES	YES
ext	object	Placeholder for exchange-specific extensions to OpenRTB.	YES	YES	YES

3.2.5 Object: Metric	Attribute	Type	Description			
	type	string; re-quired	Type of metric being presented using exchange curated string names, which should be published to bidders a priori.	No	No	YES
	value	float; re-quired	Number representing the value of the metric. Probabilities must be in the range 0.0–1.0.	No	No	YES
	vendor	string; recom-mend-ed	Source of the value using exchange-curated string names, which should be published to bidders a priori. If the exchange itself is the source versus a third party, "EXCHANGE" is recommended.	No	No	YES
	ext	object	Placeholder for exchange-specific extensions to OpenRTB.	No	No	YES

3.2.6 Object: Banner	Attribute	Type	Description			
	format	object array; recom-mend-ed	Array of format objects (Section 3.2.10) representing the banner sizes permitted. If none is specified, then the use of the h and w attributes is highly recommended.	No	YES	YES
	w	integer	Exact width in device-independent pixels (DIPS); recommended if no format objects are specified.	YES	YES	YES
	h	integer	Exact height in DIPS; recommended if no format objects are specified.	YES	YES	YES

	wmax	integer; DEP-RE-CATED	NOTE: Deprecated in favor of the format array.	YES	YES	YES
	hmax	integer; DEP-RE-CATED	NOTE: Deprecated in favor of the format array.	YES	YES	YES
	wmin	integer; DEP-RE-CATED	NOTE: Deprecated in favor of the format array.	YES	YES	YES
	hmin	integer; DEP-RE-CATED	NOTE: Deprecated in favor of the format array.	YES	YES	YES
	btype	integer array	Blocked banner ad types. Refer to List 5.2.	YES	YES	YES
	battr	integer array	Blocked creative attributes. Refer to List 5.3.	YES	YES	YES
	pos	integer	Ad position on screen. Refer to List 5.4.	YES	YES	YES
	mimes	string array	Content MIME types supported. Popular MIME types may include "application/x-shockwave-flash," "image/jpg," and "image/gif."	YES	YES	YES
	topframe	integer	Indicates if the banner is in the top frame as opposed to an iframe, where 0 = no, 1 = yes.	YES	YES	YES
	expdir	integer array	Directions in which the banner may expand. Refer to List 5.5.	YES	YES	YES
	api	integer array	List of supported API frameworks for this impression. Refer to	YES	YES	YES
List 5.6. If an API is not explic-itly listed, it is assumed not to be supported.				YES	YES	YES

	id	string	Unique identifier for this banner object. Recommended when	YES	YES	YES
	Banner objects are used with a Video object (Section 3.2.7) to represent an array of companion ads. Values usually start at 1 and increase with each object; they should be unique within an impression.			YES	YES	YES
	vcm	integer	Relevant only for Banner objects used with a Video object (Section 3.2.7) in an array of companion ads. Indicates the companion banner rendering mode relative to the associated video, where 0 = concurrent, 1 = end-card.	No	No	YES
	ext	object	Placeholder for exchange-specific extensions to OpenRTB.	YES	YES	YES

3.2.7 Object: Video	Attribute	Type	Description			
	mimes	string array; required	Content MIME types supported (e.g., "video/x-ms-wmv," "video/mp4").	YES	YES	YES

	minduration	integer; recommended	Minimum video ad duration in seconds.	YES	YES	YES
	maxduration	integer; recommended	Maximum video ad duration in seconds.	YES	YES	YES
	protocols	integer array; recommended	Array of supported video protocols. Refer to List 5.8. At least one supported protocol must be specified in either the protocol or protocols attribute.	YES	YES	YES
	protocol	integer; DEPRECATED	NOTE: Deprecated in favor of protocols .	YES	YES	YES
	w	integer; recommended	Width of the video player in DIPS.	YES	YES	YES
	h	integer; recommended	Height of the video player in DIPS.	YES	YES	YES
	startdelay	integer; recommended	Indicates the start delay in seconds for pre-roll, mid-roll, or post-roll ad placements. Refer to List 5.12 for additional generic values.	YES	YES	YES
	placement	integer	Placement type for the impression. Refer to List 5.9.	No	No	YES
	linearity	integer	Indicates if the impression must be linear, nonlinear, and so on. If none is specified, assume all are allowed. Refer to List 5.7.	YES	YES	YES

	skip	integer	Indicates if the player will allow the video to be skipped, where 0 = no, 1 = yes. If a bidder sends markup/creative that is itself skippable, the Bid object should include the attr array with an element of 16 indicating skippable video. Refer to List 5.3.	No	YES	YES
	skipmin	integer; default 0	Videos of total duration greater than this number of seconds can be skippable; only applicable if the ad is skippable.	No	YES	YES
	skipafter	integer; default 0	Number of seconds a video must play before skipping is enabled; only applicable if the ad is skippable.	No	YES	YES
	sequence	integer	If multiple ad impressions are offered in the same bid request, the sequence number will allow for the coordinated delivery of multiple creatives.	YES	YES	YES
	battr	integer array	Blocked creative attributes. Refer to List 5.3.	YES	YES	YES
	maxextend-ed	integer	Maximum extended ad duration if extension is allowed. If blank or 0, extension is not allowed. If -1, extension is allowed, and there is no time limit imposed. If greater than 0, then the value represents the number of seconds of extended play supported beyond the maxduration value.	YES	YES	YES
	minbitrate	integer	Minimum bit rate in Kbps.	YES	YES	YES
	maxbitrate	integer	Maximum bit rate in Kbps.	YES	YES	YES
	boxingal-lowed	integer; default 1	Indicates if letter-boxing of 4:3 content into a 16:9 window is allowed, where 0 = no, 1 = yes.	YES	YES	YES

	playback-method	integer array	Playback methods that may be in use. If none are specified, any method may be used. Refer to List 5.10. Only one method is typically used in practice. As a result, this array may be converted to an integer in a future version of the specification. It is strongly advised to use only the first element of this array in preparation for this change.	YES	YES	YES
	playback-end	integer	The event that causes playback to end. Refer to List 5.11.	No	No	YES
	delivery	integer array	Supported delivery methods (e.g., streaming, progressive). If none is specified, assume all are supported. Refer to List 5.15.	YES	YES	YES
	pos	integer	Ad position on screen. Refer to List 5.4.	YES	YES	YES
	companio-nad	object array	Array of Banner objects (Section 3.2.6) if companion ads are available.	YES	YES	YES
	api	integer array	List of supported API frameworks for this impression. Refer to List 5.6. If an API is not explicitly listed, it is assumed not to be supported.	YES	YES	YES
	companion-type	integer array	Supported VAST companion ad types. Refer to List 5.14. Recommended if companion Banner objects are included via the companionad array. If one of these banners will be rendered as an end-card, this can be specified using the vcm attribute with the particular banner (Section 3.2.6).	YES	YES	YES
	ext	object	Placeholder for exchange-specific extensions to OpenRTB.	YES	YES	YES

3.2.8 Object: Audio	Attribute	Type	Description			
	mimes	string array; re-quired	Content MIME types supported (e.g., "audio/mp4").	No	YES	YES
	mindura-tion	integer; recom-mend-ed	Minimum audio ad duration in seconds.	No	YES	YES
	maxdura-tion	integer; recom-mend-ed	Maximum audio ad duration in seconds.	No	YES	YES
	protocols	integer array; recom-mend-ed	Array of supported audio protocols. Refer to List 5.8.	No	YES	YES
	startdelay	integer; recom-mend-ed	Indicates the start delay in seconds for pre-roll, mid-roll, or post-roll ad placements. Refer to List 5.12.	No	YES	YES
	sequence	integer	If multiple ad impressions are offered in the same bid request, the sequence number will allow for the coordinated delivery of multiple creatives.	No	YES	YES
	battr	integer array	Blocked creative attributes. Refer to List 5.3.	No	YES	YES
	maxextend-ed	integer	Maximum extended ad duration if extension is allowed. If blank or 0, extension is not allowed. If -1, extension is allowed, and there is no time limit imposed. If greater than 0, then the value represents the number of seconds of extended play supported beyond the maxduration value.	No	YES	YES
	minbitrate	integer	Minimum bit rate in Kbps.	No	YES	YES

	maxbitrate	integer	Maximum bit rate in Kbps.	No	YES	YES
	delivery	integer	Array-supported delivery methods (e.g., streaming, progressive). If none is specified, assume all are supported. Refer to List 5.15.	No	YES	YES
	companio-nad	object array	Array of Banner objects (Section 3.2.6) if companion ads are available.	No	YES	YES
	api	integer array	List of supported API frameworks for this impression. Refer to List 5.6. If an API is not explicitly listed, it is assumed not to be supported.	No	YES	YES
	companion-type	integer array	Supported DAAST companion ad types. Refer to List 5.14. Recommended if companion Banner objects are included via the companionad array.	No	YES	YES
	maxseq	integer	The maximum number of ads that can be played in an ad pod.	No	YES	YES
	feed	integer	Type of audio feed. Refer to List 5.16.	No	YES	YES
	stitched	integer	Indicates if the ad is stitched with audio content or delivered independently, where 0 = no, 1 = yes.	No	YES	YES
	nvol	integer	Volume normalization mode. Refer to List 5.17.	No	YES	YES
	dl	integer	Indicates if the audio file can be downloaded by the user, where 0 = no, 1 = yes.	No	YES	No
	ext	object	Placeholder for exchange-specific extensions to OpenRTB.	No	YES	YES

3.2.9 Object: Native	Attribute	Type	Description			
	request	string; re-quired	Request payload complying with the native ad specification.	YES	YES	YES
	ver	string; recom-mend-ed	Version of the Dynamic Native Ads API to which request complies; highly recommended for efficient parsing.	YES	YES	YES
	api	integer array	List of supported API frameworks for this impression. Refer to List 5.6. If an API is not explicitly listed, it is assumed not to be supported.	YES	YES	YES
	battr	integer array	Blocked creative attributes. Refer to List 5.3.	YES	YES	YES
	ext	object	Placeholder for exchange-specific extensions to OpenRTB.	YES	YES	YES

3.2.10 Object: Format	Attribute	Type	Description			
	w	integer	Width in DIPS.	No	YES	YES
	h	integer	Height in DIPS.	No	YES	YES
	wratio	integer	Relative width when expressing size as a ratio.	No	No	YES
	hratio	integer	Relative height when expressing size as a ratio.	No	No	YES
	wmin	integer	The minimum width in DIPS at which the ad will be displayed the size is expressed as a ratio.	No	No	YES
	ext	object	Placeholder for exchange-specific extensions to OpenRTB.	No	YES	YES

3.2.11 Object: Pmp	Attribute	Type	Description			
	private_ auction	integer; default 0	Indicator of auction eligibility to seats named in the Direct Deals object, where 0 = all bids are accepted, 1 = bids are restricted to the deals specified and the terms thereof.	YES	YES	YES
	deals	object array	Array of Deal (Section 3.2.12) objects that convey the specific deals applicable to this impression.	YES	YES	YES
	ext	object	Placeholder for exchange-specific extensions to OpenRTB.	YES	YES	YES

3.2.12 Object: Deal	Attribute	Type	Description			
	id	string; re-quired	A unique identifier for the direct deal.	YES	YES	YES
	bidfloor	float; default 0	Minimum bid for this impression expressed in CPM.	YES	YES	YES
	bidfloorcur	string; default "USD"	Currency specified using ISO-4217 alpha codes. This may be different from bid currency returned by bidder if this is allowed by the exchange.	YES	YES	YES
	at	integer	Optional override of the overall auction type of the bid request, where 1 = first price, 2 = second price plus, 3 = the value passed in bid floor is the agreed-upon deal price. Additional auction types can be defined by the exchange.	YES	YES	YES

	wseat	string array	Whitelist of buyer seats (e.g., advertisers, agencies) allowed to bid on this deal. IDs of seats and the buyer's customers to which they refer must be coordinated between bidders and the exchange a priori. Omission implies no seat restrictions.	YES	YES	YES
	wadomain	string array	Array of advertiser domains (e.g., advertiser.com) allowed to bid on this deal. Omission implies no advertiser restrictions.	YES	YES	YES
	ext	object	Placeholder for exchange-specific extensions to OpenRTB.	YES	YES	YES

3.2.13 Object: Site	Attribute	Type	Description			
	id	string; recom-mend-ed	Exchange-specific site ID.	YES	YES	YES
	name	string	Site name (may be aliased at the publisher's request).	YES	YES	YES
	domain	string	Domain of the site (e.g., "mysite.foo.com").	YES	YES	YES
	cat	string array	Array of IAB content categories of the site. Refer to List 5.1.	YES	YES	YES
	sectioncat	string array	Array of IAB content categories that describe the current section of the site. Refer to List 5.1.	YES	YES	YES
	pagecat	string array	Array of IAB content categories that describe the current page or view of the site. Refer to List 5.1.	YES	YES	YES
	page	string	URL of the page where the impression will be shown.	YES	YES	YES

	ref	string	Referrer URL that caused navigation to the current page.	YES	YES	YES
	search	string	Search string that caused navigation to the current page.	YES	YES	YES
	mobile	integer	Indicates if the site has been programmed to optimize layout when viewed on mobile devices, where 0 = no, 1 = yes.	YES	YES	YES
	privacypol-icy	integer	Indicates if the site has a privacy policy, where 0 = no, 1 = yes.	YES	YES	YES
	publisher	object	Details about the Publisher (Section 3.2.15) of the site.	YES	YES	YES
	content	object	Details about the Content (Section 3.2.16) within the site.	YES	YES	YES
	keywords	string	Comma-separated list of keywords about the site.	YES	YES	YES
	ext	object	Placeholder for exchange-specific extensions to OpenRTB.	YES	YES	YES

3.2.14 Object: App	Attribute	Type	Description			
	id	string; recom-mend-ed	Exchange-specific app ID.	YES	YES	YES
	name	string	App name (may be aliased at the publisher's request).	YES	YES	YES
	bundle	string	A platform-specific application identifier intended to be unique to the app and independent of the exchange. On Android, this should be a bundle or package name (e.g., com.foo.mygame). On iOS, it is typically a numeric ID.	YES	YES	YES
	domain	string	Domain of the app (e.g., "mygame.foo.com").	YES	YES	YES

	storeurl	string	App store URL for an installed app; for IQG 2.1 compliance.	YES	YES	YES
	cat	string array	Array of IAB content categories of the app. Refer to List 5.1.	YES	YES	YES
	sectioncat	string array	Array of IAB content categories that describe the current section of the app. Refer to List 5.1.	YES	YES	YES
	pagecat	string array	Array of IAB content categories that describe the current page or view of the app. Refer to List 5.1.	YES	YES	YES
	ver	string	Application version.	YES	YES	YES
	privacypol-icy	integer	Indicates if the app has a privacy policy, where 0 = no, 1 = yes.	YES	YES	YES
	paid	integer	0 = app is free, 1 = the app is a paid version.	YES	YES	YES
	publisher	object	Details about the publisher (Section 3.2.15) of the app.	YES	YES	YES
	content	object	Details about the content (Section 3.2.16) within the app.	YES	YES	YES
	keywords	string	Comma-separated list of keywords about the app.	YES	YES	YES
	ext	object	Placeholder for exchange-specific extensions to OpenRTB.	YES	YES	YES

3.2.15 Object: Publish-er	Attribute	Type	Description			
	id	string	Exchange-specific publisher ID.	YES	YES	YES
	name	string	Publisher name (may be aliased at the publisher's request).	YES	YES	YES

	cat	string array	Array of IAB content categories that describe the publisher. Refer to List 5.1.	YES	YES	YES
	domain	string	Highest level domain of the publisher (e.g., "publisher. com").	YES	YES	YES
	ext	object	Placeholder for exchange-specific extensions to OpenRTB.	YES	YES	YES

3.2.16 Object: Content	Attribute	Type	Description			
	id	string	ID uniquely identifying the content.	YES	YES	YES
	episode	integer	Episode number.	YES	YES	YES
	title	string	Content title. Video Examples: "Search Committee" (television), "A New Hope" (movie), or "Endgame" (made for Web). Non-video example: "Why an Antarctic Glacier Is Melting So Quickly" (Time magazine article).	YES	YES	YES
	series	string	IAB Technology Lab Content series. Video examples: "The Office" (television), "Star Wars" (movie), or "Arby 'N' The Chief" (made for web). Non-video example: "Ecocentric" (Time Magazine blog).	YES	YES	YES
	season	string	Content season (e.g., "Season 3").	YES	YES	YES
	artist	string	Artist credited with the content.	No	YES	YES
	genre	string	Genre that best describes the content (e.g., rock, pop, and so on).	No	YES	YES
	album	string	Album to which the content belongs; typically for audio.	No	YES	YES

	isrc	string	International Standard Recording Code conforming to ISO-3901.	No	YES	YES
	producer	object	Details about the content producer (Section 3.2.17).	YES	YES	YES
	url	string	URL of the content, for buy-side contextualization or review.	YES	YES	YES
	cat	string array	Array of IAB content categories that describe the content producer. Refer to List 5.1.	YES	YES	YES
	prodq	integer	Production quality. Refer to List 5.13.	No	YES	YES
	videoqual-ity	integer; DEP-RE-CATED	Note: Deprecated in favor of prodq .	YES	YES	YES
	context	integer	Type of content (game, video, text, and so on). Refer to List 5.18.	YES	YES	YES
	contentrat-ing	string	Content rating (e.g., MPAA).	YES	YES	YES
	userrating	string	User rating of the content (e.g., number of stars, likes, and so on).	YES	YES	YES
	qagmedi-arating	integer	Media rating per IQG guidelines. Refer to List 5.19.	YES	YES	YES
	keywords	string	Comma-separated list of keywords describing the content.	YES	YES	YES
	livestream	integer	0 = not live, 1 = content is live (e.g., stream, live blog).	YES	YES	YES
	sourcerela-tionship	integer	0 = indirect, 1 = direct.	YES	YES	YES
	len	integer	Length of content in seconds; appropriate for video or audio.	YES	YES	YES
	language	string	Content language using ISO-639-1-alpha-2.	YES	YES	YES

	embeddable	integer	Indicator of whether or not the content is embeddable (e.g., an embeddable video player), where 0 = no, 1 = yes.	YES	YES	YES
	data	object array	Additional content data. Each Data object (Section 3.2.21) represents a different data source.	No	YES	YES
	ext	object	Placeholder for exchange-specific extensions to OpenRTB.	YES	YES	YES

3.2.17 Object: Producer	Attribute	Type	Description			
	id	string	Content producer or originator ID. Useful if content is syndicated and may be posted on a site using embed tags.	YES	YES	YES
	name	string	Content producer or originator name (e.g., "Warner Bros").	YES	YES	YES
	cat	string array	Array of IAB content categories that describe the content producer. Refer to List 5.1.	YES	YES	YES
	domain	string	Highest level domain of the content producer (e.g.,"producer.com").	YES	YES	YES
	ext	object	Placeholder for exchange-specific extensions to OpenRTB.	YES	YES	YES

3.2.18 Object: Device	Attribute	Type	Description			
	ua	string; recom- mend- ed	Browser user agent string.	YES	YES	YES

	geo	object; recommended	Location of the device assumed to be the user's current location defined by a Geo object (Section 3.2.19).	YES	YES	YES
	dnt	integer; recommended	Standard "Do Not Track" flag as set in the header by the browser, where 0 = tracking is unrestricted, 1 = do not track.	YES	YES	YES
	lmt	integer; recommended	"Limit Ad Tracking" signal commercially endorsed (e.g., iOS, Android), where 0 = tracking is unrestricted, 1 = tracking must be limited per commercial guidelines.	YES	YES	YES
	ip	string; recommended	IPv4 address closest to device.	YES	YES	YES
	ipv6	string	IP address closest to device as IPv6.	YES	YES	YES
	devicetype	integer	The general type of device. Refer to List 5.21.	YES	YES	YES
	make	string	Device make (e.g., "Apple").	YES	YES	YES
	model	string	Device model (e.g., "iPhone").	YES	YES	YES
	os	string	Device operating system (e.g., "iOS").	YES	YES	YES
	osv	string	Device operating system version (e.g., "3.1.2").	YES	YES	YES
	hwv	string	Hardware version of the device (e.g., "5S" for iPhone 5S).	YES	YES	YES
	h	integer	Physical height of the screen in pixels.	YES	YES	YES
	w	integer	Physical width of the screen in pixels.	YES	YES	YES
	ppi	integer	Screen size as pixels per linear inch.	YES	YES	YES
	pxratio	float	The ratio of physical pixels to DIPS.	YES	YES	YES
	js	integer	Support for JavaScript, where 0 = no, 1 = yes.	YES	YES	YES

	geofetch	integer	Indicates if the geolocation API will be available to JavaScript code running in the banner, where 0 = no, 1 = yes.	No	YES	YES
	flashver	string	Version of Flash supported by the browser.	YES	YES	YES
	language	string	Browser language using ISO-639-1-alpha-2.	YES	YES	YES
	carrier	string	Carrier or ISP (e.g., "VERIZON") using exchange curated string names, which should be published to bidders a priori.	YES	YES	YES
	mccmnc	string	Mobile carrier as the concatenated MCC-MNC code (e.g., "310-005" identifies Verizon Wireless CDMA in the USA). Refer to https://en.wikipedia.org/wiki/Mobile_country_code for further examples. Note that the dash between the MCC and MNC parts is required to remove parsing ambiguity.	No	No	YES
	connection-type	integer	Network connection type. Refer to List 5.22.	YES	YES	YES
	ifa	string	ID sanctioned for advertiser use in the clear (i.e. not hashed).	YES	YES	YES
	didsha1	string	Hardware device ID (e.g., IMEI); hashed via SHA1.	YES	YES	YES
	didmd5	string	Hardware device ID (e.g., IMEI); hashed via MD5.	YES	YES	YES
	dpidsha1	string	Platform device ID (e.g., Android ID); hashed via SHA1.	YES	YES	YES
	dpidmd5	string	Platform device ID (e.g., Android ID); hashed via MD5.	YES	YES	YES
	macsha1	string	MAC address of the device; hashed via SHA1.	YES	YES	YES
	macmd5	string	MAC address of the device; hashed via MD5.	YES	YES	YES

	ext	object	Placeholder for exchange-specific extensions to OpenRTB.	YES	YES	YES

3.2.19 Object: Geo	Attribute	Type	Description			
	lat	float	Latitude from -90.0 to +90.0, where negative is south.	YES	YES	YES
	lon	float	Longitude from -180.0 to +180.0, where negative is west.	YES	YES	YES
	type	integer	Source of location data; recommended when passing lat/lon . Refer to List 5.20.	YES	YES	YES
	accuracy	integer	Estimated location accuracy in meters; recommended when lat/lon are specified and derived from a device's location services (i.e., type = 1). Note that this is the accuracy as reported from the device. Consult OS-specific documentation (e.g., Android, iOS) for exact interpretation.	No	YES	YES
	lastfix	integer	Number of seconds since this geolocation fix was established. Note that devices may cache location data across multiple fetches. Ideally, this value should be from the time the actual fix was taken.	No	YES	YES
	ipservice	integer	Service or provider used to determine geolocation from IP address if applicable (i.e., type = 2). Refer to List 5.23.	No	YES	YES
	country	string	Country code using ISO-3166-1-alpha-3.	YES	YES	YES
	region	string	Region code using ISO-3166-2; 2-letter state code if USA.	YES	YES	YES

	Attribute	Type	Description			
	region-fips104	string	Region of a country using FIPS 10-4 notation. While OpenRTB supports this attribute, it has been withdrawn by NIST in 2008.	YES	YES	YES
	metro	string	Google metro code; similar to but not exactly Nielsen DMAs. See Appendix A for a link to the codes.	YES	YES	YES
	city	string	City using United Nations Code for Trade and Transport Locations. See Appendix A for a link to the codes.	YES	YES	YES
	zip	string	Zip or postal code.	YES	YES	YES
	utcoffset	integer	Local time as the number +/- of minutes from UTC.	YES	YES	YES
	ext	object	Placeholder for exchange-specific extensions to OpenRTB.	YES	YES	YES

3.2.20 Object: User	Attribute	Type	Description			
	id	string; recommended	Exchange-specific ID for the user. At least one of id or buyeruid is recommended.	YES	YES	YES
	buyeruid	string; recommended	Buyer-specific ID for the user as mapped by the exchange for the buyer. At least one of buyeruid or id is recommended.	buy-erid	YES	YES
	yob	integer	Year of birth as a four-digit integer.	YES	YES	YES
	gender	string	Gender, where "M" = male, "F" = female, "O" = known to be other (i.e., omitted is unknown).	YES	YES	YES
	keywords	string	Comma-separated list of keywords, interests, or intent.	YES	YES	YES

	customdata	string	Optional feature to pass bidder data that was set in the exchange's cookie. The string must be in base85 cookie-safe characters and be in any format. Proper JSON encoding must be used to include "escaped" quotation marks.	YES	YES	YES
	geo	object	Location of the user's home base defined by a Geo object (Section 3.2.19). This is not necessarily their current location.	YES	YES	YES
	data	object array	Additional user data. Each Data object (Section 3.2.21) represents a different data source.	YES	YES	YES
	ext	object	Placeholder for exchange-specific extensions to OpenRTB.	YES	YES	YES

3.2.21 Object: Data	Attribute	Type	Description			
	id	string	Exchange-specific ID for the data provider.	YES	YES	YES
	name	string	Exchange-specific name for the data provider.	YES	YES	YES
	segment	object array	Array of Segment (Section 3.2.22) objects that contain the actual data values.	YES	YES	YES
	ext	object	Placeholder for exchange-specific extensions to OpenRTB.	YES	YES	YES

3.2.22 Object: Segment	Attribute	Type	Description			
	id	string	ID of the data segment specific to the data provider.	YES	YES	YES
	name	string	Name of the data segment specific to the data provider.	YES	YES	YES
	value	string	String representation of the data segment value.	YES	YES	YES
	ext	object	Placeholder for exchange-specific extensions to OpenRTB.	YES	YES	YES

4.1 Object Model	Object	Section	Description			
	BidResponse	4.2.1	Top-level object.	YES	YES	YES
	SeatBid	4.2.2	Collection of bids made by the bidder on behalf of a specific seat.	YES	YES	YES
	Bid	4.2.3	An offer to buy a specific impression under certain business terms.	YES	YES	YES

Index

Printed in Great Britain
by Amazon

11209688R00120